Measuring Instructional Results

or Got a Match?

Second Edition

Robert F. Mager

Lake Publishing Company
Belmont, California

BOOKS BY ROBERT F. MAGER

Preparing Instructional Objectives, *Revised Second Edition*

Measuring Instructional Results, *Second Edition*

Analyzing Performance Problems, *Second Edition*
(with Peter Pipe)

Goal Analysis, *Second Edition*

Developing Attitude Toward Learning, *Second Edition*

Making Instruction Work

Developing Vocational Instruction
(with Kenneth Beach)

Troubleshooting the Troubleshooting Course

Library of Congress Catalog Card Number: 83–60502
Printed in the United States of America

2.9 8

Contents

Preface

Once upon a time, as the crow flies, the king of Hairmania decided to shave off his beard.

"It is an event that will bring attention and fame—not to mention tourists," he beamed. "Bring the Royal Barber."

"But sire," lamented his advisor, "there isn't one. No one has shaved for a hundred years."

"Hairesy!" exploded the king. "No wonder we're so crowded. Sally ye forth, therefore, and find me the best in all the land."

Which he did. And when at last the most famous barber was found, he was sent to the Royal Three Committees for the Royal Testing.

"Tell us about the history of barbering," asked the first committee.

And he did.

"Tell us about the importance of barbering," asked the second committee.

And he did.

"Tell us what instruments you would use to shave the king," asked the third committee.

And he did.

Whereupon they draped his neck with their Medallion of Approval and led him before the king. Wasting no time, the barber prepared his tools and spread his cloth. But when he picked up his razor with a swirling flourish—he accidentally sliced a piece off the king's ear.

"Gadzooks!" cried the king. "You've cut off my royal ear!"

"Ooops," chorused the nine voices of the Royal Three Committees.

"Oops?" astonished the king. "I ask for skill and you give me oops?"

"We're very sorry," apologized the Royal Three Committees. "We must have lost our heads."

"A capital idea," rejoiced the king, and sprang himself forth to make it permanently so.

And ever since and forever more,
There hang nine heads on the Royal Door.
For this was the fate of the Committees Three . . .
May it never befall such as me . . . or thee.

And the moral of this fable is
HE WHO ASKS WRONG QUESTIONS MAY LOSE
MORE THAN FACE.

When it is important that one's instruction be successful, it would also seem important to bestir oneself to determine whether one has succeeded as intended. The measurement of instructional success is accomplished mainly through the development of test items (situations, performance items, simulations, role-play, paper-pencil, etc.) that precisely match each objective in scope and intent. This book is designed for those who want to know how well their instruction works and how to develop the basic tools with which to measure instructional results. It shows how to recognize or prepare test items through which one can determine whether an instructional objective has been achieved.

We do not weigh steam with a yardstick or evaluate music with a bathroom scale. Such measures would be irrelevant to the things being measured. Similarly, we do not measure achievement of objectives with test items that do not match those objectives. If you can identify a test item that is right for testing an objective, you will have most of the skill needed to prepare your own items. My intent is to offer you a procedure and practice items that will help you to do just that. Specifically, the objective of the book is this:

> *Be able to discriminate* (select, point to) *the test items that are appropriate (i.e., items that match the objective in performance and conditions) for testing the achievement of an instructional objective, when given (1) an objective, (2) one or more allegedly suitable test items, and (3) the Objective/Item Checklist.*

The checklist just mentioned is provided as an aid to carrying out the matching procedure, so it will not be necessary to memorize the steps of that procedure (see page 59 and the card inserted between the last page and the back cover). Once you know *how* each step works, the checklist can be used to remind you *when* each may be applicable.

Three comments before we begin. First, most of the objectives you will encounter will need at least some repair before you can select or prepare items to match. Therefore, examples of these kinds of objectives are included to make the practice items more useful.

Second, we are concerned here only with matching objectives and test items, and consequently we will not deal with the characteristics of either one that aren't relevant to the job at hand. For example, we will not deal with the usual test item construction issues of item difficulty or the structure of multiple-choice or true-false items. At that, the book offers more of a beginning than an end—the intent is more to get you started than to try to solve the advanced problems. But a beginning is important. After all, it is useless to complain that the advanced problems haven't been solved while one is still screwing up the fundamentals.

Finally, when an objective is being drafted, it is not always known whether it will ultimately be judged important enough to be achieved. For that reason, many objectives come into being that aren't really important. And when you see an objective that isn't important, that is, when it doesn't matter whether it is achieved, you should not only not bother to write or select test items that are appropriate to the objective—you shouldn't test at all.

And so, to begin.

ROBERT F. MAGER

Carefree, Arizona
January, 1984

1 || What It's All About

Suppose you had been working hard during a course to achieve this objective handed you by the instructor on the first day:

On a level paved street, be able to ride a unicycle one hundred yards without falling off.

Suppose you had strengthened your thighs with deep-knee bends, and had practiced riding until you could mount and ride with relative ease for at least *two* hundreds yards. And suppose that when testing time came around, your instructor asked you to get out pencil and paper and answer the following questions:

1. Define *unicycle*.
2. Write a short essay on the history of the unicycle.
3. Name at least six parts of the unicycle.
4. Describe your method of mounting a unicycle.

What would be your reaction? How would you feel if you had been told to learn one thing and were then tested on another?

Equally important, perhaps, would the instructor find out whether the objective had been achieved?

Suppose the instructor "justifies" this situation to you with one or more of the following comments. How would you feel?

"We don't have the facilities to give performance tests."

"We don't have enough unicycles to go around."

"This is an educational institution, not a training institution."

"It doesn't matter how well you can ride; if you don't know anything about the unicycle you can't really appreciate it."

"I'm teaching for transfer."

"It's too easy to learn to ride a unicycle; I have to add some harder items so I can grade on a curve."

"If everybody learned to ride, I'd have to give everybody an A."

"I like to vary the type of items I use to make my tests interesting."

"I want my tests to be a learning situation."

"I'm teaching creativity and insight."

"I have to design my tests so they can be machine scored."

"Students should learn by discovery."

Regardless of the truth or falsity of the comments listed above, the fact remains that you can*not* find out whether a person can ride a unicycle unless you or someone else watches that person ride one. You cannot find out if the objective is achieved unless you use items that ask the student to perform whatever the objective is about. If you use items that aren't "right" for an objective, not only will you *not* find out if your objective is achieved, you may fool yourself into thinking it is. That's not so bad when an objective isn't very important, but when it *matters* whether it is achieved, you run a risk by using poorly conceived or inappropriate items. If it matters whether the patient's temperature is less than 100 degrees, you'd better use a thermometer to measure his or her temperature rather than a yardstick . . . or an essay. If it matters whether a student pilot can react quickly and accurately in a stall emergency, then you'd better use a reaction-producing item rather than a yardstick . . . or an essay. If it matters whether a student is able to read at least two hundred words per minute, then you'd better find out if that skill can be performed, so you can respond with

○

more instruction when it can't or with applause when it can, rather than with merely a student label (i.e., a grade).

THE VIEW FROM THE TOP

In theory, the development of items that test for an objective is straightforward and a simple matter for those whose objectives are derived from task analyses and are well stated. (Those who have objectives of this kind may not realize that they are among a small minority, and may well wonder how so much can be said about what to them is only "common sense.") One merely has to prepare items that ask the student to demonstrate the performance called for by the objective, under the conditions called for by the objective. In other words, one prepares items in which the performance and conditions match those of the objective to be assessed. In practice, this preparation is only a little more difficult then the telling.

However, the main difficulties do not arise from problems in item writing. Most difficulties are caused by the objectives. Often, when test items are drafted to match an objective, the objective itself exists in only a crude or sloppy state. If, for example, no performance at all is mentioned in the statement *called* an objective, test items cannot be written until the objective is repaired.

Another important obstacle to easy preparation of test items arises from the tendency of instructors to consider the student fair game for almost any kind of test. This tendency somehow gives instructors a feeling of uneasiness when they construct test items strictly according to the objective. "These items don't cover enough ground," the feeling says. "These items are too easy," it tells them and makes them conveniently forget that the object is not to develop a variety of items that only half the students can master, but to *prepare items that will reveal which students can perform as desired.* And the feeling goes on to say, "Well, maybe students can perform as well or better than expected, but they won't *really* understand it unless . . ." and then urges instructors to add all sorts of test items having little or no relation to the objective. Finally, this funny feeling, in a last desperate bid for survival, says, "Well, maybe all the students *have* achieved the objective, but you need to add some harder items so you can spread them out on a curve."

Because the objectives we see and use vary considerably in their precision, I will be using comparable statements (of varying precision) in the examples that follow. We need to learn to handle the world as it is; it is hardly useful to learn to handle an ideal that seldom appears.

As for that funny feeling that urges us to use almost any form of test item so long as it "covers" the material presented, the best I can do to help you avoid that feeling is to describe the reasons for the present approach and to try to help you develop skill in implementing it. After all, *people who know how to do something are more likely to do it than those who don't!!* And if they know *why* they are doing it they may feel more at ease when they *are* doing it.

WHAT'S TO COME

The next chapter will describe a few distinctions in terms, so we will have a better basis for communication. After that there will be discussion and practice in locating and interpreting ("decoding") the key characteristics of an objective. Then there will be discussion and practice in matching performances, followed by practice in matching conditions. Next, if you like, you can practice repairing some items to match the objectives they are supposed to be related to, before going on to some practice in the entire skill. Finally, if you should desire to test *my* skill, there is a set of test items that allegedly matches the objective of this book.

Here and there along the way you will be encouraged to skip the sections that describe things you may already know. There is no sense in spending time going over what you can already do.

The use of inappropriate test items is a widespread phenomenon and is, in my opinion, a practice (malpractice?) most urgently in need of improvement. When we deceive the student by discrepancies between our words and our deeds, both sides are the losers. Putting it more plainly, when we cheat students, they generally find a way to cheat back.

2 || Distinctions

A number of distinctions will serve as the basis for the following chapters, and it will be useful to describe these distinctions at least briefly. If we both use words in a similar manner, the words won't get in the way of the ideas; these descriptions won't take long to go through, and they should help to put a few ideas in their proper place.

ITEMS AND TESTS

Perhaps the main distinction to make is between tests and test items. If you've ever spent much time in a school you couldn't avoid either one, so this distinction may appear obvious. It is mentioned, however, as a way to remind you that this book is concerned mainly with test *items* rather than with tests.

Item: A test item calls for a single response or set of responses to a single stimulus or stimulus pattern. It is one sample of a behavior or performance. That performance may be simple, as when asking someone to write the answer to an addition problem, or it may be complex, as when asking someone to perform an appendectomy, analyze a problem, or compose a sonata.

Test: A test is an event during which someone is asked to demonstrate some aspect of his or her knowledge or skill. Though a test can consist of a single test item, a test generally consists of several items.

MEASUREMENT, EVALUATION, AND GRADING

Measurement: The process of measurement determines the extent of some characteristic associated with an object or person. For example, when we determine the length of a room or the weight of an object, we are measuring.

Evaluation: The act of evaluation compares a measurement with a standard and passes judgment on the comparison. We are making evaluations when we say things like—it's too long, it's too hot, he's not motivated, she's too slow, he's honest. We have noted the extent of some characteristic, compared it with some standard, and then passed judgment on the comparison.

A test is a way of *measuring* some desired characteristic. We pose a situation or problem and note a response. The shape or extent of the response provides the basis for the measurement. Thus, when we say that "seven out of ten of the student's responses were correct," we are noting the extent of an ability to respond to that kind of question or problem. We are using a test as a measuring device. On the other hand, when we then say things such as

"She passed"

"He flunked"

"She's not working up to her potential"

"He's good enough"

we are making evaluations. We have compared the results of the measurement with some standard (real or imagined, stable or shifting) and have made a judgment.

The difference between measurement and evaluation can be illustrated with this two-line dialogue:

"Hey, these watermelons are three feet long." (measurement)

"Wow!"   (evaluation)

Or it can be illustrated with this example:

"This student can type thirty words per
minute."   (measurement)
"That's too slow."   (evaluation)

Grading: A grade is a label representing an evaluation. Sometimes that evaluation is based on measurement and sometimes on guesses, intuition, expectation, or bias. Traditionally, a grade has intended to say something about how well a student has performed (or tried) *in relation to his or her peers;* it has meant that the student is very good, pretty good, about the same as, not as good as, or poorer than those who happen to be his or her classmates. Also traditionally, the student has seldom been informed of the precise basis for the grade.

In this book we are concerned with the issue of measurement, with offering a sound basis for determining whether an objective has been accomplished.

NORM-REFERENCED AND CRITERION-REFERENCED EVALUATION

Norm-referenced: When the performance of one student is compared with that of other students, and a judgment is passed on the basis of that comparison, a norm-referenced evaluation is being made. Thus, when we say that student X is above average and that student Y is below average, we are making a norm-referenced evaluation. When we rank-order students on the basis of their performance in *reference to each other,* we are making norm-referenced evaluations. Grading on a curve is such an evaluation. So is the assignment of IQ.

If we have five automobiles, none of which runs, we might measure the extent of their defects and say "Automobile G 'doesn't run' the best. None of them goes, but G is the best of non-goers." That would be a norm-referenced evaluation. If we then said, "Give that car an A+," we would be grading on the basis of a norm-referenced evaluation.

Criterion-referenced: When we compare a measurement not with other measurements, but with some objective standard, we are making a criterion-referenced evaluation. If we measure our automobiles and say "None of them runs," we have compared the state of each car with the criterion of movement and judged that none meets that criterion.

The difference between the norm-referenced and criterion-referenced methods of evaluation was beautifully illustrated a few years ago by an example called "The Coffee Pot,"* and it went like this. Imagine that an objective said that a student is to be able to make a pot of coffee. He or she has all the necessary tools and equipment, and the task is to make a pot of coffee. A checklist of each of the steps in the process is prepared, and the student's performance is scored on both a norm-referenced and a criterion-referenced basis. Look at the Checklist for Making a Pot of Coffee and the scores. Note the difference between the two methods of scoring.

Checklist for Making a Pot of Coffee

	NORM-REFERENCED SCORING	CRITERION-REFERENCED SCORING
Disconnects coffee pot	10	√
Disassembles coffee pot	10	√
Cleans components and pot	10	√
Inspects components	10	√
Fills pot with water	10	√
Reassembles components	10	√
Fills basket with coffee	0	X
Reconnects coffee pot	10	√
Sets dial on coffee pot	10	√
Reports pot is perking properly	10	√
SCORE	90%	0%

---

* Example and Checklist courtesy of Dr. James Whipple.

Note that in a norm-referenced system a student can accumulate a score of 90 percent, *even though he or she failed to make a pot of coffee.* A criterion-referenced system, on the other hand, gives the same student a score of zero. Though most of the skills were acquired, the objective was not accomplished. By failing to demonstrate the making of a pot of coffee, a student cannot be certified as having achieved the objective.

In regard to instruction, criterion-referenced evaluation refers to comparing a student's performance with a desired standard and judging whether the student did or did not meet or exceed the standard. For example, suppose we expect a student to be able to spell 60 percent of the words in Booklet 3 correctly, and he or she spells 56 percent of them correctly. When we say that the student has spelled 56 percent correctly, we are describing the results of a measurement. Now there are two kinds of evaluation that can follow:

Norm-referenced: "Gee, this performance is the best in the class. Give the student an A."

Criterion-referenced: "This performance did not meet the criterion of 60 percent. Give the student more instruction."

Though there are some uses for norm-referenced evaluation, the concern here will be with criterion-referenced evaluation. When we want to know *whether* an expectation (objective) or criterion has in fact been achieved, only criterion-referenced procedures are appropriate.

CRITERION ITEMS AND DIAGNOSTIC ITEMS

Criterion item: An item that is designed to help us determine whether some criterion has been achieved.

Diagnostic item: An item that is designed to tell us something about why a criterion has NOT been achieved.

For example, if we wanted to find out if someone could bake a pie that met certain standards, we would use a *criterion item* designed for that purpose. We would ask someone to bake a pie. If that person could do it, and if the pie met the standards set for it, we would say that the criterion had been met. He or she could bake a pie.

If, however, the pie did not get made at all, or if the finished pie oozed to the floor in a puddle, we would say that the would-be baker did not meet the criterion. When this is the case, we may want to know *why* the person did *not* meet the criterion, why he or she couldn't do the task. Items designed to find out why a criterion was *not* achieved are called *diagnostic items*.

The distinction is important. A test often contains both criterion items and diagnostic items; many contain *only* diagnostic items. If we do not know the difference between the two, *we run the risk of evaluating whether a student has achieved a criterion by looking at his or her performance on a diagnostic item.* Thus, if we want to know if a student can peel an orange, we should make that judgment on the basis of the criterion item (e.g., "Let me see you peel that orange"), and NOT on the basis of a diagnostic item (e.g., "Tell me *how* you would peel that orange." or "Is this an orange?").

The criterion item provides the proof of the pudding but doesn't help much with the recipe. A simple depiction of the uses of the two types of items is shown in the sketch. Although some criterion items can be useful for diagnostic purposes, the

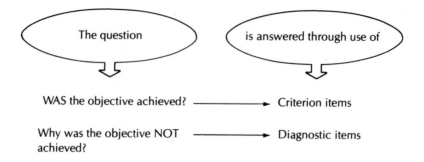

The question   is answered through use of

WAS the objective achieved? ————▶ Criterion items

Why was the objective NOT ————▶ Diagnostic items
achieved?

emphasis in this book will be with the criterion item as the means of determining whether an objective has been accomplished. More will be said about this topic in Chapter 6.

INSTRUCTIONAL OBJECTIVES AND CRITERION TEST ITEMS

Instructional Objectives: These statements are descriptions of intended *results* of instruction. They are descriptions of the standards we would like students to achieve or surpass.

Criterion Test Items: These are the measures used to find out whether objectives have been achieved. They are designed to match the objective closely so that this evaluation can be made: Has the objective been accomplished?

Sometimes the criterion item looks very much like the objective. For example,

Objective: *Be able to bake a pie.*

Criterion Item: *Here are some utensils and ingredients. Bake a pie.*

But often it does not—

Objective: *Be able to solve word problems.*

Criterion Item: *John is twice as old as Sue. If John is three years older than his ten-year old dog, how old is Sue?*

To qualify as a criterion item, an item must match the objective in (1) performance and (2) conditions. The purpose of this book is to show you how to make that match.

3 | Decoding the Objective

Many procedures are more difficult to explain than to perform. For example, imagine explaining the tying of a shoelace, the addition of a column of numbers, or the playing of a sonata. In each case the skill can be performed faster than the explanation of it—once the skill has been learned. In some cases the learning is relatively easy, in some cases more difficult. But the explaining takes longer than the doing.

So it is with the procedure for writing or selecting test items relevant to the assessment of an objective. The explaining and the learning take longer than the doing; enough longer to make the point worth mentioning. To make sure we don't lose sight of our purpose along the way, I may occasionally repeat this rule:

Write or select items that will ask students to do what the objective says they are to be able to do.

Basically, the entire procedure is one of noting aspects of the objective, noting aspects of the test item, and then deciding if they are the same or different. If these aspects are the same, the item may be useful in determining whether that objective has been achieved; if they are different, the item must be modified or discarded. Since the first thing to do is to look at the objective, that is where we will begin. Once you get used to decoding the objective, you will be able to decode almost instantaneously.

STEP ONE. Note the performance stated in the objective.

This means no more than to note the word or phrase that tells what the students will be doing when demonstrating their achievement of the objective. Most of the time this is easy to do. Sometimes it is more difficult, partly because of a gray area between what a performance is and what an abstraction is, and partly because the "objective" may not mention any performance at all.

Let's look at a few simple examples, just to be sure we are thinking about the same thing.

Draw a circle around the explicit *performance,* if any, mentioned in the following statements.

1. Be able to write the symbols for any twenty electronic components.

2. Be able to demonstrate an understanding of modern poetry.

3. Be able to multiply pairs of two-digit numbers.

4. Be able to show a knowledge of the basic elements of a contract.

Turn the page to check your responses.

1. Be able to (write the symbols) for any twenty electronic components.

2. Be able to demonstrate an understanding of modern poetry.

3. Be able to (multiply) pairs of two-digit numbers.

4. Be able to show a knowledge of the basic elements of a contract.

In the first item, the performance mentioned is writing the symbols. That's what it says. Never mind for the moment whether *writing* is what the objective is really all about. For the moment we are only concerned with what the statement asks the student to do.

The second item has *no* performance. *Demonstrate* doesn't qualify. What would someone be doing when demonstrating an understanding? Running? Jumping? Writing? Explaining? We can't tell. The word demonstrate *sounds* like a performance, but that's all.

The third item asks the student to multiply. That's what it says. Since you can find out directly whether someone did or did not multiply correctly, multiplying would qualify as a performance, as would similar intellectual skills.

The last item mentions no performance at all. Thus, it may qualify as a goal, but in its present form it doesn't make it as an objective.

If you had any difficulty at all with these items, you could use a little practice in recognizing the difference between performances and abstractions.   *Turn to page 19.*

If you breezed through the practice items   *Turn to page 23.*

Performances and Abstractions. Performances are *specific* things that people say and do. People can *demonstrate* a performance. They sing, they write papers, they type, they point to things. These are performances.

People also solve problems, compare things, and recall the steps in procedures. These are also called performances, even though you can't see the actions directly. They're called performances because they are actions initiated by people at will to accomplish something specific. And, because you can tell whether people are doing (or have done) these things by asking them to demonstrate *one* visible or audible thing. You can find out whether a problem has been solved by asking the solvers to write the answer. You can find out whether people recalled the steps of a procedure by asking them to recite the steps to you.

Performances are what objectives are about.[1]

Sometimes, however, people say things *about* other people that *describe their condition, their state of being.* These are abstractions. For example, if we see someone lying on a desk, we may say, "She's lazy." Now *lazy* isn't a performance. It's a word describing an alleged state of being, a condition someone might be in. It's an abstraction in the sense that it is an attempt to generalize about a person's state of being from observing behavior. Words like *nice, genial,* and *studious* and expressions such as "they have a poor attitude," and "he's not motivated" talk *about* people, rather than describe something that they are doing.

---

1. For more help in sorting out objectives, read *Preparing Instructional Objectives, Revised Second Edition,* R. F. Mager (David S. Lake Publishers, 1984).

For instance, all of the following examples would qualify as performances:

Go and . . .   add these numbers
                    ride this bike
                    solve this problem
                    identify the smallest letters
                    play this song
                    divide these numbers
                    describe the characters

These examples would *not* qualify as performances:

Go and . . .   internalize your growing awareness
                    be happy
                    think clearly
                    demonstrate your understanding

The key point is whether you can tell directly whether the performance occurred to your satisfaction. Is there one kind of behavior a person could exhibit to let you know he or she has performed as desired? Would there be general agreement that this behavior does reflect what was wanted? If so, you have a performance. If not, you are dealing with an abstraction. (*If you can't tell, don't make a big thing out of it;* if there is a disagreement about whether an item is calling for a performance or stating an abstraction, simply have the one who wrote the objective modify it.)

For example, is there one thing you could ask a person to do to let you know he or she has solved a problem correctly? Would other people generally agree? If so, consider *solving* as a performance. Is there one thing you could ask someone to do to let you know he or she appreciates literature? Would others agree? If they would want someone to exhibit a different behavior from the one you have selected, or a *number* of behaviors, think of *appreciation* as an abstraction.

Now try the following examples.

Circle the performance, if any, mentioned in these statements.

1. Without a musical score, sing a chorus of any of the songs on the following list (list would be added here).

2. Be able to know the principles of behavior modification.

3. Be able to demonstrate an understanding of the principles of aerodynamics.

4. Be able to take and record blood pressure for an adult patient of any size or weight.

5. Be able to describe the procedure for completing a ballot used in a national election.

Check your responses on the following page.

1. Without a musical score, (sing a chorus) of any of the songs on the following list (list would be added here).

2. Be able to know the principles of behavior modification.

3. Be able to demonstrate an understanding of the principles of aerodynamics.

4. Be able to (take and record blood pressure) for an adult patient of any size or weight.

5. Be able to (describe the procedure) for completing a ballot used in a national election.

The performance mentioned in the first item is *singing.* You can tell if someone is doing that. You can tell directly.

There is no performance mentioned in Items 2 and 3. You are not told what the student is expected to do. Or, you can think of it this way: whoever reads these statements will have to *guess* what the statements mean.

Can you tell if someone is *taking* or *recording* blood presssure? Sure you can. Call it a performance.

Can you tell if someone is *describing*? Yes, so describing qualifies as a performance.

To repeat, the first step in selecting test items that are appropriate to an objective is to note the performance mentioned in the objective. If none is mentioned, ask the writer of the objective to fix it.

If *no* performance is mentioned, the statement isn't an objective and you won't be able to select test items that match. If no performance is mentioned, you must either get clarification from whoever wrote the statement, clarify it yourself, or throw it away. Without a performance stated, there is little sense going to the next step in selecting items.

After you have noted the performance, you are ready for the second step.

Step One. Note the performance stated in the objective.

STEP TWO. Note whether the performance is the main intent or an indicator.

If the performance stated in an objective always described the *main thing* the objective is about, we wouldn't have any trouble reading an objective. We'd just look at the performance that was stated and say, "OK, this is about being able to _____." It would be as simple as that.

Unfortunately, the objectives you will find in the real world aren't written that way. In some objectives the performance stated *is* the main intent, the main thing the objective is about.

In others, the performance stated is what we call an *indicator behavior*. Instead of telling us what the objective really wants someone to be able to do, it tells us *how we are going to find out* whether he or she can do what the objective is really about. It names an indicator behavior through which we can assess the main intent.

Here's an example. Suppose the objective says:

> *Given a collection of business letters, be able to make a check mark on those conforming to company policy as outlined in the Perfect Policy Manual of 1993.*

What performance is *actually stated?* Make a check mark. That's what it says. But is *that* the main intent of the objective? Does the objective writer expect to teach people how to go around making check marks on business letters? Hardly. So what is the objective really about? What is the main intent of the objective? Discriminating, that's what. Being able to tell the difference between letters that do and don't meet the standards stated in the manual.

Therefore, here is an objective that has a performance stated, but the performance is *not* the main intent of the objective. In this case we can easily detect what the main intent is (it isn't always this easy), and say, "The performance stated is an indicator; the main intent is discriminating."

Consider these examples:

Given a fully equipped surgery, be able to perform a lobotomy on any breed of dog.

Question one: What is the performance mentioned in the objective? *Performing a lobotomy.* That's what it *says.*

Question two: What is the main intent of the objective? What is the objective mainly about? Why, it is about being able to perform a lobotomy. There is no reason to suspect otherwise. Lobotomizing is the skill the learner is expected to develop.

In this example the performance stated in the objective is the main intent of the objective. Knowing that, we also know that the only way we can find out if someone has accomplished the objective is to ask that person to perform a lobotomy. (Asking students to make check marks on lobotomies might tell us if they can recognize one when they see one, but it won't tell us if they can perform one.)

Now let's ask the same two questions of this statement:

Given a series of pictures depicting animals and non-animals, be able to color all the animals.

Question one: What is the performance stated in the objective? *Coloring.* That's what it *says*.

Question two: What is the main intent? What is the objective all about? What does it want learners to be able to do? Why, the objective wants them to be able to tell the difference between animals and non-animals. It doesn't *say* so, but in this case it is clear that this is the main intent. So the answer to "What is the main intent?" here is "Discriminate *(recognize, differentiate)* between animals and non-animals."

Then why does the objective say *color* when it wants learners to be able to discriminate? Simply because in this case the objective writer decided to state an indicator rather than a main intent. Ideally, the objective would state the main intent *and* the indicator when an indicator is needed. In this case it doesn't. So this is another example in which the performance stated is an indicator, and the main intent is implied.

There is nothing wrong with having an objective state an indicator behavior and not the main intent, *so long as the main intent is clear.* In fact, you'll see that an indicator behavior is absolutely essential in some cases. For the moment let's just concentrate on the difference between the main intent and the indicator.

Main intent (primary intent, principal purpose) is the performance that is the purpose of the objective.

Indicator behavior is an activity through which the existence of the main intent will be inferred.

In the example on recognizing animals, you are told to infer from the student's coloring behavior whether he or she can tell the difference between animals and non-animals. Since you can tell what the main intent is, and since you know that the main intent is not coloring, you know you are not going to teach the student to color merely because that is the performance stated in the objective. You also know that it would be an error on your part if you evaluated or graded the student on his or her coloring ability (i.e., you would never say a thing such as "Yes, you can tell the difference between animals and non-animals, all right, but you did a sloppy job of coloring so I'll have to take 10 points off."). The objective isn't about coloring, it is about discriminating. Coloring is just an indicator of the main intent. Since the main intent is clear, I wouldn't bother to rewrite the objective; I'd leave it as is and simply make sure I didn't evaluate the quality of the coloring when evaluating achievement of the main intent.

To check your skill at identifying main intents and indicators, try the items noted on the next page.

Circle the performance stated, and then check (√) the appropriate column to the right. Is the *stated* performance an indicator or a main intent?

	MAIN INTENT	INDICATOR
1. Be able to identify the verb in any sentence.	___	___
2. Be able to circle a verb in any sentence.	___	___
3. Given a number of one-dollar bills, be able to mark those that are counterfeit.	___	___
4. Given a group of essays and a set of standards, be able to evaluate the essays according to the standards.	___	___

Check your responses on the following page.

	MAIN INTENT	INDICATOR
1. Be able to (identify the verb) in any sentence.	✓	___
2. Be able to (circle a verb) in any sentence.	___	✓
3. Given a number of one-dollar bills, be able to (mark those that are counterfeit.)	___	✓
4. Given a group of essays and a set of standards, be able to (evaluate the essays) according to the standards.	✓	___

1. What does the first statement want the learner to be able to do? It wants him or her to be able to *identify* verbs. That is the main intent. There is no indicator and so you don't know *how* you will know that the identifying was accomplished, but it seems pretty clear that identifying is a main intent.

2. The second statement mentions *circle* as the performance. But is that what it is all about? No, circling is an indicator through which you will find out if the main intent, probably identification, has been accomplished.

3. The third item says *mark,* but it is clear that the main intent is for someone to be able to recognize a counterfeit one-dollar bill when he or she sees it.

4. The statement wants the student to be able to *evaluate* essays according to a set of standards. That's what it says. It doesn't tell us, or even suggest, what visible behavior will be acceptable as evidence of evaluating, but it seems clear that evaluating is the main intent. If you think evaluating is an abstraction rather than a performance, follow the rule. Don't make a big thing out of it; either fix it yourself or get the writer to fix it.

When you have noted whether the stated performance is the main intent or an indicator, you are ready for the next step.

Step One. Note the performance stated in the objective.

Step Two. Note whether the performance is the main intent or an indicator.

STEP THREE. If the performance is an indicator, note the main intent.
If the performance is the main intent, note whether it is overt or covert.

Let's consider each part of this step separately.

If the performance is an indicator, note the main intent.

By definition, an indicator behavior is one that is used as a basis from which to infer the presence or absence of something else. In the case of an objective, the indicator is used as the basis for inferring whether the main intent of the objective has been achieved. But it is possible to select indicators that are *un*suitable as well as suitable. It is possible that the indicator selected is not the best one for the job. *If you can't identify the main intent of an objective, you can't judge whether the indicator will indicate what you want it to indicate.*

Therefore, it is important to be able to identify the main intent so that you will be able to complete the next step of comparing the indicator with the main intent to make sure it is a suitable indicator. No sense writing or selecting test items that call for performance that won't tell you what you want to know.

If, when reading the objective, you are able to identify the main intent, fine. That's all there is to the step. If not, you will need to ask the objective writer for clarification. For example, in the following statement it is clear that the performance called for is an indicator. But what is the main intent?

Given any page of non-technical prose, be able to circle dangling participles.

Why should one be able to circle these things? Surely a person isn't expected to go around the world circling danglers. Circling is just an indicator that shows a learner can do something meaningful. But what? Perhaps he or she is expected to be able to recognize or identify dangling participles. That would be my guess. But I could be wrong. It may be that the objective writer wants a learner to be able to write grammatically correct sentences, and is using the circling as a means of finding out whether he or she can do so. The point is simply that we are not *sure* what the main intent of the objective is. Whenever this is the case, ask the objective writer to make a revision. Don't sit around stewing about whether a word is or isn't an abstraction; don't waste time taxonomizing. If you can't tell easily what the objective is all about, ask or fix. The example on dangling participles might be rewritten as follows:

> *Given any page of non-technical prose, be able to identify dangling participles by circling them.*

Or,

> *In examples of non-technical prose, be able to identify dangling participles.*
> Sample test item: *Circle all the dangling participles on the attached page of non-technical prose.*

If the performance is the main intent, note whether it is overt or covert.

If the performance is a main intent and is mainly visible (overt), then you are ready to move to the test item to see if it matches.

But if the performance is a main intent and is *not* visible—that is, if the main intent is cognitive, internal, or mental (covert)—then a suitable indicator needs to be added before items can be matched. Always.

Until now we have talked of performances in terms of whether they are main intents or indicators. But we also talk of performances in terms of whether they are overt or covert. We see in Figure 1, therefore, that a performance can be:

1. An overt (visible or audible) main intent
2. A covert (invisible) main intent
3. An overt (visible or audible) indicator

Figure 1

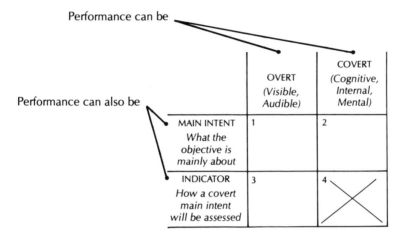

In Figure 1, the box representing "covert indicator" is crossed out because that category is an absurdity. An indicator cannot indicate anything if it is invisible.

> Performances that are directly visible or audible are called *overt*. Examples are writing, marking, singing, kicking, and screaming. (Indicators are always overt.)

> Performances that are not directly visible, those that are carried out somewhere inside you, are called *covert*. Examples are identifying, recalling, solving, adding.

Most performances have both covert and overt elements, but you are concerned only with whether the performance is *mainly* overt or covert. Riding a bicycle is mainly a visible performance, even though there are things going on in your head (or someplace) when you are riding. Writing is mainly visible, even though there are some covert activities going on at the same time. Adding, on the other hand, is mainly a covert performance. Observers can't see you adding. They may be able to tell that you are adding by watching your lips move or your eyebrows twitch, but lip moving and eyebrow twitching are not the performance of adding. If you can do something without moving any of your movable parts, you are performing a covert act.

And if you can add (or identify) in your head without moving a muscle, how will other people know you did it? Why, you tell them. Or you write something down. Or you punch some buttons or underline something. These are all ways of indicating that a covert act has been performed. The indicators are not the covert performance, but unless some kind of indicator is used you will never know if the covert act was performed to your satisfaction.

So when the performance stated in the objective is a *covert main intent*—that is, when the main thing the objective is all about is not directly visible—then you need to add a suitable indicator to the objective before proceeding. How do you do that? Well, the easiest, fastest thing to do is simply to leave the objective the way it is and to add a sample test item to the objective. This way, you will avoid the business of fussing with the wording, and, at the same time, you will be telling the learner what he or she will need to do to demonstrate achievement of the main intent.

For example, the following statement contains a covert main intent; before you can match test items to it, you need to know what will be a suitable indicator.

Given a list of statements describing (1) goals and (2) performances, identify the performances.

Rather than bother with the wording of the objective, let's add a sample test item to it, as suggested. The learner will then know what he or she will have to do to demonstrate achievement, and you will be provided with a sounder basis for selecting items for the criterion test. Try it this way:

Given a list of statements describing (1) goals and (2) performances, identify the performances. Example: Consider the following statements, and check those that are performances.

> *(a) Make a boat.*   ____
> *(b) Consider the problem.*   ____
> *(c) Think clearly.*   ____

Now the statement has an indicator to go along with the main intent, so we know how the objective writer expects to find out if the main intent has been achieved. But it is possible to select *bad* indicators as well as *good* indicators; it is possible to select indicators that are *wrong* for the task they are expected to perform. How do you tell whether an indicator is a good one? By testing the indicator. And that's the next step.

But first . . .

If you are not sure of your ability to label performances as either overt or covert, a little practice would be in order.

A little practice wouldn't hurt   **page 35**

Let's move on   **page 37**

Overt performance is behavior that you can see or hear.

Covert performance occurs inside a person, but it is detectable through overt behaviors. A covert performance is something you can detect through a *single type* of visible behavior.

Below are a few words describing various actions. Some are directly visible and some are not. Check (√) those that are directly visible or audible, those about which you can say, "When people are doing that, I can see or hear them doing it."

1. State   ____

2. Acquire   ____

3. Write   ____

4. Draw   ____

5. Recognize   ____

6. Add   ____

7. Solve   ____

8. Recall   ____

Check your responses on the following page.

1. State	✓	4. Draw	?	7. Solve	___
2. Acquire	?	5. Recognize	___	8. Recall	___
3. Write	✓	6. Add	___		

1. Overt. You can tell if someone is stating something. (Or abstract, as a picky manuscript tester pointed out, if "state of mind" is being referred to.)

2. Covert or overt, depending on what is being acquired. Acquiring a concept is covert; acquiring a wallet is overt. (Words can be sneaky, can't they?)

3. Overt. You can tell directly when someone is writing.

4. Overt or covert. Drawing a picture is overt; drawing conclusions is covert. (Don't blame me for the fact that words don't always have a single meaning or implication.)

5. Covert. For you to be able to tell whether someone *recognized,* he or she would have to do something other than recognize—such as point a finger, say something, or write a note.

6. Covert. I've already discussed this one. What if the person's adding on a machine, you say? Isn't the adding overt then? I suppose so, and perhaps there should be a question mark beside that item above. Notice the care that must be taken if you are to be clear.

7. Covert. But again, similar to adding. One could be said to be solving problems when inserting data into a computer, I suppose. The machine would be doing the information manipulation, but the operator would be said to be solving.

8. Covert. I can recall all sorts of things and not let anyone know I am doing it. If you want to know if someone has recalled something, you need an indicator—an overt behavior that will signal the recalling.

Continue to the next page.

To this point you've looked at the objective to note whether it states a performance, and if so, whether that performance is the main intent of the objective or an indicator behavior through which achievement of the main intent will be determined. You have noted whether a main intent is overt or covert. You have noted that an objective with a covert main intent must have an indicator behavior.

For those objectives that contain an indicator, there is only one more step to complete before moving on to take a look at the test item. That step is included so that you can make sure your indicators will do what they are supposed to do. You test the indicators. You check to make sure they are simple and direct so that they don't muddy your search in determining if your objective has been achieved to your satisfaction. This is Step Four, given on the next page.

Step One. Note the performance stated in the objective.

Step Two. Note whether the performance is the main intent or an indicator.

Step Three. If the performance is an indicator, note the main intent. If the performance is a main intent, note whether it is overt or covert.

STEP FOUR. For objectives containing an indicator, test the indicator.

To *test the indicator* simply means to ask this question about the indicator:

Is this indicator the simplest and most direct I can find, and is it well within the repertoire of the student?

If the answer is yes, then the indicator behavior is probably all right to use. If the answer is no, the indicator needs to be changed.

Let me illustrate the point with this nutty dialogue.

You: What are you doing there?

Me: Well, you see, I've got this large piece of paper sitting on this table, and I've been measuring how much the paper has been contracting over the past few minutes.

You: Why are you doing that?

Me: Why, to find out how warm it is, of course. Paper contracts in heat.

You: Why don't you use a thermometer?

Me: That's too easy. *Anyone* could do *that*.

My method of finding out the temperature was far more complex than necessary, and wouldn't really tell me what I wanted to know. That's why we test our indicators—to make sure they are as simple as possible and give us the information we want.

Consider this example, borrowed from an English teacher:

Demonstrate an understanding of the difference between an epic and a sonnet by writing one of each.

Now watch closely (nothing up my sleeve, and at no time do my fingers leave my hands).

Question one: What's the performance stated in the objective? *Writing.* That's the doing word.

Question two: What is the covert main intent of the objective? What is it mainly about? Well, it is about being able to tell the difference between epics and sonnets. That's what it says. The main intent is one of discrimination. (It doesn't say *what kind* of differences the student should be able to discriminate, but it clearly implies that "being able to tell the difference" is the main intent.)

Question three: If the main intent is to find out if students can tell the difference between epics and sonnets, how will the instructor know if they can do it? Why, the instructor will ask them to *write* one of each. It is clear that writing an epic and a sonnet is the indicator by which the objective writer intends to tell if the main intent is achieved.

Asking students to *write* sonnets and epics to find out whether they can tell them apart seems a bit much, don't you think? Isn't there an easier, more direct indicator that can be used? Something that will tell us whether students can recognize epics and sonnets when they see them, and something that will *not* require students to do *more* than tell us they can recognize the difference? Of course. There are several alternatives.

We could give students a pile of pages, each of which has an epic or sonnet on it, and ask students to *sort* the pages into two piles—one pile for epics and one for sonnets. *Anyone* ought to be able to sort pages. Or, we could ask them to poke a pencil through the epics. Or, we could ask them to make a check mark on the sonnets. Or any number of simple, direct actions (behaviors) that anyone could be expected to perform. Each of these indicators would tell us whether the desired discrimination is taking place; each of them would directly assess the main intent of the objective, *without* making it easy to mistakenly assess something *other* than the main intent. And that is why it is important to test an indicator—to make sure it is the one that will assess a main intent and not something else. If the indicator asks for more behavior than is needed to assess a main intent, you run the risk of confusing assessment of the main intent with an assortment of the indicator behavior. In the example of the epics and sonnets that means there is a strong possibility that an instructor will evaluate students on their ability to write epics and sonnets, and think he or she is evaluating their ability to tell the difference between them.

"Well," you might hear this instructor say to a student, "sure you can tell the difference between epics and sonnets, but you write a lousy sonnet and so I'm going to have to take 20 points off."

Or, "Well, you can tell one from another, but you don't *really understand* the difference until you can write one." Balderdash! When the indicator isn't the simplest, most direct one possible, and if it isn't well within the repertoire (present capability) of the student, the evaluation of the main intent of the objective will almost invariably be confounded with an evaluation of the student's performance of the indicator.

How often have you heard things like this—

"Well, you got the problems right but your handwriting is terrible."

"Your essay said all I wanted it to, but I'll have to mark you down for grammar."

Each such sentiment suggests that academic sneakery is about to be perpetrated.

If you make sure that an indicator is simple, direct, and well within the ability of the student to perform, you will minimize the chance that you will be measuring something other than the thing you want to measure—namely, the main intent of the objective.

Here, then, is how you make sure:

1. Note the covert main intent of the objective. If there isn't any, or if you can't tell what it is, you can't select or improve upon indicators that will tell you whether the main intent has been achieved. Fix the objective.

2. When the covert main intent is clear, ask whether there is a simpler, more direct way to assess its achievement. If there is, fix the indicator. If not, you're ready to move on to the selection of test items.

That's all there is to it.

Except for one point. *Any* indicator will do if it is simple, direct, and well within the ability of the student. In the example of the epics and sonnets, checkmarking sonnets would be as direct as circling epics. Each of these indicators is a simple behavior from which we can *directly infer* whether the covert main intent has been achieved.

So when the main intent of the objective is covert, the indicator behaviors used to assess achievement of the objective must be simple, direct, and well within the repertoire of the student. In addition, ANY indicator that is simple, direct, and well within the repertoire of the student will do, provided it allows us to make a direct inference about whether the main intent has been accomplished.

When an objective has an overt main intent, such as running, typing, interviewing, or repairing, then *no* indicator is needed. In this instance you determine whether the main intent has been accomplished by asking students to perform the main intent itself. There's no other way.

Let's nail down Step Four with a few practice items.

Practice in Testing the Indicator.   On the next page are some objectives with covert main intents and some form of indicator. To ease your reading burden, I've left off detailed conditions and criteria.

Circle the indicator.

If the indicator is the simplest, most direct one you can think of, check YES.

If not, check NO, and write a more appropriate one in the space provided.

OBJECTIVE	YES	NO	WRITE A BETTER INDICATOR

1. Demonstrate an ability to recognize counterfeit money by accepting the bills and completing procedures listed under Section 20 of the Operations Manual, "Counterfeit Money."   ___ ___

2. Be able to identify sentences that are statements of bias, assumption, generalization, or conclusion, by writing the sentences under those categories.   ___ ___

3. Be able to compute the solution to binary addition problems.

   Sample test item: Describe the steps in the solution of each of the following binary addition problems:

11000	0101
11000	0011

       ___ ___

4. Be able to identify the function of each of the keys of a 10-key calculator by using each key appropriately when solving a series of problems.   ___ ___

Turn the page to check your responses.

OBJECTIVE	YES	NO	WRITE A BETTER INDICATOR

1. Demonstrate an ability to recognize counterfeit money by accepting the bills and completing procedures listed under Section 20 of the Operations Manual, "Counterfeit Money."
       ___   ✓   Sort bills

2. Be able to identify sentences that are statements of bias, assumption, generalization, or conclusion, by writing the sentences under those categories.   ___   ✓   Circle the category

See explanation of these responses on the next page.

Here's Why

1. Main intent: discriminating counterfeit money
   Indicator: completing procedures required when counter-
        feit money has been accepted
   Simplest, most direct indicator? No.

In this instance the indicator is not only more difficult than required, it is not related to the main intent. The main intent is to have students able to recognize counterfeit money when they see it. A suitable indicator would be to have students sort money into two piles—counterfeit and genuine. Or to have them write the letter associated with, or to point to, counterfeit bills displayed among real ones on a board. In any case, the most direct indicator is one that asks students to *point to* counterfeit bills in the simplest way possible. And the behavior selected for the indicator must be well within the repertoire of the students. You wouldn't ask them to write anything, for example, unless they write *with ease*.

2. Main intent: discriminating statements of bias, etc.
   Indicator: writing the sentence
   Simplest, most direct indicator? No.

In this example the stated indicator would let you know whether the objective has been achieved. But though the indicator is a direct one, it is by no means the simplest one. It asks students to do more than needed to indicate their ability to recognize the types of sentences asked for. It asks students to *write* a sentence when the objective only wants to know if they can *recognize* a sentence. There are several indicators that would be less bulky and less demanding of student time, and that would tell you directly whether the discriminating occurred as desired. For example, four columns could be drawn to the right of the sentences to be judged, each headed with one of the four judgment categories (i.e., bias, assumption, generalization, conclusion). Students could be asked to read

(Continued on page 47.)

3. Be able to compute the solution to binary addition
problems.

Sample test item: (Describe)
(the steps) in the solution of
each of the following bi-
nary addition problems:

11000	0101
11000	0011

___ ✓   Write the solution

4. Be able to identify the
function of each of the
keys of a 10-key calcula-
tor by (using each key) appropriately when solving
a series of problems.

___ ✓   Check the function

2. *(Continued)*

each sentence presented and to *check* the appropriate column. That would be much simpler than writing the sentence under a category; it would tell you what you want to know more directly. Or, students might be asked to write the name of the category next to the sentence. While that entails more writing than checking does, it would be considerably simpler than writing the sentence.

3. Main intent: solving problems

 Indicator: describing steps

 Simplest, most direct indicator? No.

In this example the main intent and the indicator clearly do not match. It is not possible to determine whether students can solve problems by asking them to describe the steps they would follow in solving the problems. Oh, sure, if they can't describe the steps, you might conclude with some confidence that they can't solve the problems. But if they *can* describe the steps, you cannot conclude that they *can* solve the problems. Describing isn't the same as solving.

How can you tell whether students have solved an addition problem correctly? Why, ask them to tell you the solution. Or ask them to write the solution. Either indicator would be direct and simple. If you were interested in *how* they arrived at their solution, some other indicator would be called for. The objective, however, is interested in solutions, not procedures.

4. Main intent: identifying functions

 Indicator: using keys

This example is more difficult to deal with because it is not easy to tell what the objective means by identify. If it means that students are to be able to tell or describe the function or use of each key, then telling or describing would be the way to get at the main intent. If it means that students are to be able to

(Continued on next page.)

4. *(Continued.)*

recognize the function of each key, then you might point to a key and have a student point to a statement that describes its function. If it means that students should be able to use each key correctly, then the indicator as stated is okay, but the objective should be reworded.

True, the statement is ambiguous; but I've included it because it represents examples you will have to deal with. You might as well start excruciating over this sort of thing along with the rest of us.

Watch out whenever the word *identify* is used in an objective, because it is a real sleeper of a problem. You see, everyone who uses the word knows what *he or she* means by it. The problem is that everyone *doesn't* realize that other people may have different meanings for the same word. For example, *identify* is sometimes used to mean "point to," as in "Identify the bones of the body." In one case it might mean to point to bones on a diagram; in other cases it might mean to point to the real thing. Then again, *identify* is used to mean "select a verbal description of the real thing," as in "Identify the correct answers in each of these multiple-choice questions." The word is also used to mean "describe or tell," as in "On the paper provided, briefly identify the causes of bankruptcy." Finally, it is sometimes used to mean "list," as in "Identify the steps in cashing a check." With all these possible meanings floating around, the word *identify* cannot be accepted as an indicator; when it is a main intent, it must be accompanied by its intended meaning.

WHERE WE ARE

At this point you should be able to carry out the steps associated with decoding the objective. That is, when looking at an objective, you should be able to:

1. Note the performance stated.
2. Note whether the performance is a main intent or an indicator.
3. Note whether or not a main intent is clear and whether it is overt or covert.
4. Test an indicator for its simplicity.

Once you can carry out these steps, you are ready to begin matching test items to objectives—to see if the items will tell you whether the objective has been achieved as you intended.

And that's just what comes next.

4 | Matching the Performances

"So the way you find out how many cows there are in the pasture is to count the number of legs and divide by four."

"Why not just count heads directly?"

"Because if you're off a few legs, you're not off that many cows."

Dumb, isn't it? About as dumb as my trying to find out how well you write by asking you to answer some multiple-choice questions about writing. About as dumb as trying to find out if someone can *interview* by asking them to *point to* errors in other peoples' interviews. Unless the measuring instrument matches the thing to be measured, we just haven't got a chance of learning what we want to know.

At this point what we want to know is whether or not an objective has been achieved. To find out we ask someone to *do* whatever it is the objective is about. To do that we create what we call a "test item" to ask for the doing. So, to zero in on what we want to know, we need only make sure that the test item asks for the same doing as the objective. That's what this chapter is about. Remember our rule:

Write or select items that will ask students to do what the objective says they are to be able to do.

Most of the time the act of checking whether the performance of a test item matches that of an objective takes only a second or so, provided the objective is well stated. Only when the objective is poorly stated, or when the main intent of the objective is covert (invisible), does it take a few seconds longer.

Here's the basic procedure:

1. Circle the performance stated in the objective. (If none is stated there is nothing to circle, and you can stop right here, as you can't match something to nothing.)
2. Circle the performance asked for by the test item. (Actually circling the performances makes it easier to see whether or not they are the same.)
3. If they're the same, go on to match the conditions. If they're different, the item isn't appropriate for telling you whether the objective has been achieved.

To clarify what to do, let's consider each of these two situations: (1) the overt performance stated is the main intent; and (2) the overt performance stated is an indicator.

The Overt Performance Stated in the Objective Is the Main Intent.   When the visible performance stated in the objective is the *main intent* of that objective, then the performance of the item is matched to the main intent. That is, in this case there is nothing to do but prepare or select test items that ask students to *perform the main intent of the objective*. No indicator is needed; no indicator is appropriate. In other words, when the performance in the objective is overt and is the main intent, *then there is only one type of test item on the face of the earth suitable for testing achievement of that objective*. Whatever the objective says for students to do, the item must ask them to do it. No other form of item is acceptable. For example, if the objective says

> *Be able to ride a unicycle 100 yards on a level paved surface without falling off.*

the performance stated is *riding*. The performance of riding is overt and is what the objective is all about. Therefore, the only way you can find out if learners achieved the objective is to ask them to *ride*. No other form of test item is appropriate, regardless of how interesting it is and regardless of the "difficulty level." You cannot find out if students can ride a unicycle by asking them questions on the history of spokes, by asking them to write essays on seat appreciation, or by having them answer multiple-choice questions on nomenclature. The only way you can find out if they can ride is to watch them ride.

Now, you may want them to ride successfully three times out of four before you will say the objective is achieved (provided that criterion is called for by the objective), and in that sense you would have four items or behavior samples. But each and every one of them MUST ask students to ride. If it asks them to do anything else, you will *not know* whether the objective is achieved.

Consider this example:

> *Be able to pick open any four of six given five-pin tumbler locks within twenty minutes.*

What's the performance stated? Picking locks. Is the performance visible? Yes. You can see people picking locks. What is the main intent? Why, lock picking. The objective wants students to be able to open locks of a certain kind by picking them. To find out whether students can do that, should I use *any* of the following items?

1. Draw a diagram of a typical pin tumbler.
2. For a five-pin tumbler lock, name the picks you would use in picking it open.
3. Name three people important to the history of the pin tumbler.
4. For each of the locks named on the list below, write the name of the picks most appropriate for speedy opening.
5. Write a short essay on the history of keyholes.

No sir! Not a one of those items is appropriate if you want to find out whether students can actually pick. And to include items like these just because they may make the test more interesting is not playing fair with students. It is simply no good to have items that ask them to pick a little, talk a little. It's got to be pick, pick, pick, or you will never know if the objective has been achieved. And if you don't know whether it has been achieved, you won't be able to show that your instruction is as successful as you think it is.

So, when the performance mentioned in the objective is OVERT and at the same time the MAIN INTENT, the test item is just about the same as the objective, because it must call for exactly the performance stated in the objective. (Not so incidentally, it is because of this type of objective that some people mistakenly conclude that there is no difference between objectives and test items. *That is true only in the case where the main intent of the objective is overt.* In all other instances it is NOT true, and those who say otherwise are leading you astray.)

The Overt Performance Stated in the Objective Is an Indicator. In this case the main intent of the objective is covert (if it weren't, there would be no call for an indicator behavior). Here are the things to do:

1. Note the main intent of the objective.
2. Make sure the indicator stated is the simplest and most direct indicator possible. If so, proceed. If not, fix or have fixed.
3. Note the performance called for by the test item.
4. Is that performance the *same*, or the same *type*, as the indicator stated in the objective?
   - If so, go on to check the conditions.
   - If not, modify or discard the test item.

Let's look at an example.

Objective: Be able to identify (underline) *verbs in a series of sentences.*

Question one: What's the *visible* performance stated? *Underlining.*

Question two: Is that the simplest, most direct indicator? Yes. It's one of several that might be used, but it is simple, direct, and well within the student's ability.

Test item: *There are ten sentences on this page. Circle the verb in each.*

Question three: What's the performance called for in the test item? *Circling.*

Question four: Is that the same, or the same type of performance, as underlining? Yes. Underlining and circling are two simple ways to *point to* the verbs. Each requires the same amount of skill (or lack of it).

So in this example the performance called for by the test item is the "same" as that of the objective, and the item is suitable for assessing achievement of the objective. All that remains is to make sure the conditions match, which we'll do in the next chapter.

Here's another example.

Objective: *From an array of watchmaking tools, be able to identify those used for winding mainsprings.*

Test item: *Each of the tools laid out on Table 2 has been numbered. On your answer sheet, write the number of each of the tools used for winding mainsprings.*

Question one: What's the *visible* performance stated in the objective? *There isn't any.* Identifying is a covert performance. So before proceeding we must add an indicator. After a second or two of thought, we revise the objective as follows:

Objective: *From an array of watchmaking tools, be able to identify* (point to) *those used for winding mainsprings.*

Notice how easy it is to improve the objective by adding a word or two in parentheses, rather than by rewriting the entire statement. Now we have a visible performance and can go on to the next question.

Question two: Is this a simple, direct indicator? Yes. Everyone has *something* they can point with.

Question three: What's the performance called for in the test item? *Writing* a number.

Question four: Is that the same, or same type, of performance as pointing? Close, but no cigar. *If* the target audience (students) can write numbers easily and legibly, then writing numbers would be OK for an indicator behavior. Can you think of an even simpler indicator to use? One that wouldn't require even a writing skill? How about the following as possibilities?

- Put the tools used for mainspring winding in the green tray.
- Remove the tags from the correct tools and hand them to the instructor.
- Point to the tools used for mainspring winding.

One more example.

Objective: Given any number of completed interview forms, select (checkmark) *those that meet the standards listed in the Guide to Quality Employees.*

Test Item: List characteristics an applicant must have to meet the standards described in the Guide to Quality Employees.

OK, let's have at it.

Question one: What's the *visible* performance stated in the objective? *Checkmarking.* That's what it says.

Question two: Is that a simple, direct indicator of selecting? Yes.

Question three: What's the performance called for in the test item? *Listing.*

Question four: Is listing the same as checkmarking? Not even close.

"But," you will hear people say, "if students don't know what the characteristics *are* that applicants must have, they won't be able to select the forms that meet the standards." Probably true. But that's irrelevant, isn't it? The point is that if you want to find out whether students have accomplished the objective, you have to ask them to perform as the objective describes. That is, to find out whether students can select proper interview forms, you need to ask them to do just that. Not write essays about them, or answer multiple-choice questions about them. Students should be asked to perform as desired, not to demonstrate what they would need to *know* before performing as desired.

In this example, then, the performances called for in the test item and the objective do not match. One or the other needs to be fixed.

By now you should be ready for some practice in matching performances, and so some guided practice is coming up. To help you with your matching, I'll offer three kinds of aids. Take your pick.

WHAT-TO-DO SUMMARY

Figure 2

	OVERT	COVERT
MAIN INTENT	1 *Match main intent*	2 *ADD and match indicator*
INDICATOR	3 *Match indicator*	4

When the performance stated in the objective is:

1. Main intent and overt

There is only one type of test item that will do. Ask the student to do that which is called for by the objective.

2. Main intent and covert

Add an indicator to the objective: test to make sure it is simple, direct, and well within the repertoire of the student. Write or select test items that call for the same or a similar indicator behavior.

3. Indicator and overt

Check the main intent. If unclear, fix or discard the objective. If clear, make sure that the indicator is appropriate — simple, direct, and well within student capability. Write or select test items that call for the same or a similar indicator behavior.

4. Indicator and covert

No such thing. Say something tart to the objective writer. Get the objective fixed or junked.

*Objective/Item Checklist**

1. What performance is stated in the objective?

2. What is the performance?

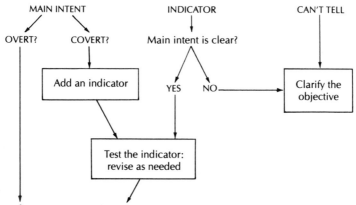

3. What overt performance is asked for by the objective?

4. What performance is asked for by the item?

5. Do the performances match?

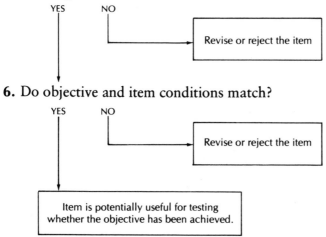

6. Do objective and item conditions match?

* Courtesy of Mager Associates, Inc. (A removable copy of this checklist is inserted between the last page and back cover of this book.)

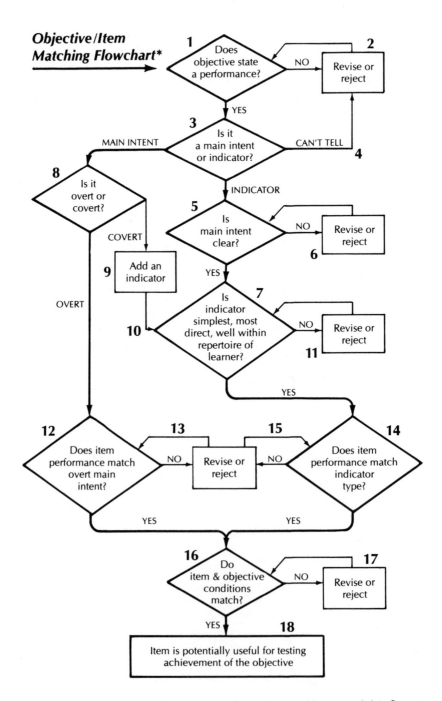

Objective/Item Matching Flowchart*

1 Does objective state a performance?

2 Revise or reject — NO

YES

3 Is it a main intent or indicator?

MAIN INTENT

CAN'T TELL **4**

8 Is it overt or covert?

INDICATOR

5 Is main intent clear?

6 Revise or reject — NO

COVERT

YES

9 Add an indicator

10

OVERT

7 Is indicator simplest, most direct, well within repertoire of learner?

11 Revise or reject — NO

YES

12 Does item performance match overt main intent?

13 Revise or reject — NO

15 NO

14 Does item performance match indicator type?

YES

YES

16 Do item & objective conditions match?

17 Revise or reject — NO

YES

18 Item is potentially useful for testing achievement of the objective

* Courtesy of Mager Associates, Inc. (A removable copy of this flow-chart is inserted between the last page and back cover of this book.)

EXPLANATION OF FLOWCHART STEPS

The following brief explanation is numbered according to the numbers shown on the flowchart to the left.

1. What is the performance stated in the objective?

2. If there isn't any, repair or discard the objective.

3. Is the performance a main intent or an indicator?

4. If you can't tell, revise or discard the objective.

5. If it is an indicator, can you tell what the main intent is?

6. If you can't, revise or discard the objective.

7. If you can, test the indicator against the main intent.

8. If the performance is a main intent, is it overt or covert?

9. If covert, add an indicator.

10. Test the indicator for simplicity.

11. If needed, revise or reject.

12. If the performance is overt, does the item performance match?

13. If not, revise or reject item or objective.

14. If performance is an indicator, does the item performance match?

15. If not, revise or reject item.

16. Do the conditions described in the item match those of the objective?

17. If not, revise item.

18. If so, item is potentially useful for testing whether the objective has been achieved.

GUIDED PRACTICE

Here are some practice items that will let you try your hand at matching performances, when they are stated.

Each pair of statements consists of an objective and a test item. You are asked to decide YES or NO, according to whether the performance called for by the test item matches that called for by the objective. If you CAN'T TELL whether there is a match because the objective or item doesn't call for a performance, check (√) the CAN'T TELL column.

Note: You will find it considerably easier to decode the problems if you will actually *circle the performances* with your pencil as you go. That way the verbiage won't get so much in the way. If there is nothing to circle in the way of a performance, it doesn't matter how profound the statement sounds; check CAN'T TELL and go on to the next item.

On the chance that you will be able to move through the practice in a more sprightly manner if I model the procedure, I will invite you to peer into my stream of consciousness as I work through the first practice item.

1. *Objective:* Given a customer deposit to either a savings or checking account, be able to verify the deposit. (Verify means count the cash, compare amount of cash with amount shown on deposit slip, check deposit slip calculations for accuracy, stamp and initial deposit slip after verification.)

   Criterion Item: Describe how you would respond to this customer comment: "I'd like to make a deposit to my checking account but I don't know how to fill out these new deposit slips. What do I have to do to deposit $20.00 in cash and a check for $14.79?"   ____   ____   ____

Thoughts While Matching. "Let's see, now. What's the performance called for by the objective? Well, it says *verify the deposit.* I'll circle that so it won't get away. Now. Is that the main intent or an indicator? Actually, it looks like the main thing the objective is about. The student is expected to be able to verify deposits when he or she leaves the instruction. Okay, so the performance is a main intent. Is it overt or covert? Hmmm. Looks like some of both, but it seems mainly visible. I could watch someone verifying deposits directly.

"Okay, the performance stated in the objective is an overt main intent. That tells me that there is only one kind of item that will do—one that asks the student to verify deposits. So let's look at the test item. What does it ask the student to do? It says *describe a response to a customer comment.* Oh, oh. Describing a response isn't the same as verifying a deposit. The performances don't match, so I'll put a check in the NO column." (In practice you would discard or repair the item rather than check a column.)

Now it's your turn to try a few.

2. *Objective:* Be able to construct a staircase according to given blueprints and specifications.

   Criterion Item: Inspect these blueprints and specifications and decide whether they were properly followed in the construction of the staircase labeled Staircase 3.   —— ——   ——

3. *Objective:* Support a candidate of your choice in his or her campaign for election to a public office.

   Criterion Item: Prove that you have supported a candidate of your choice in his or her campaign for election to a public office.   —— ——   ——

4. *Objective:* Be able to carry out the booking procedure for an adult violator of any section of the Penal Code that requires taking the subject into custody.

   Criterion Item: George Spelvin, age 23, male, has been caught in the act of setting fire to an office building (Section 448a, PC). Complete all the steps needed to book the subject.   —— ——   ——

5. *Objective:* Embark on a life-long search for truth, with the willingness and ability to pose questions, examine experience, and construct explanations and meanings.

   Criterion Item: Read *Wisdom from the Mountain* and describe its meaning to you in relation to your life goals.   —— ——   ——

6. *Objective:* Be able to identify and mark circuit design errors on circuit diagrams of transistor amplifiers.

Criterion Item: Envelope B contains two circuit diagrams of transistor amplifiers. These diagrams contain errors consisting of either missing components, extra components, or components connected in wrong places. Draw a circle around each error you find.   ____   ____   ____

Turn the page to check your responses.

1. *Objective:* Given a customer deposit to either a savings or checking account, be able to verify the deposit. (Verify means count the cash, compare amount of cash with amount shown on deposit slip, check deposit slip calculations for accuracy, stamp and initial deposit slip after verification.)

   Criterion Item: Describe how you would respond to this customer comment: "I'd like to make a deposit to my checking account but I don't know how to fill out these new deposit slips. What do I have to do to deposit $20.00 in cash and a check for $14.79?"

   ___ ✓ ___

2. *Objective:* Be able to construct a staircase according to given blueprints and specifications.

   Criterion Item: Inspect these blueprints and specifications and decide whether they were properly followed in the construction of the staircase labeled Staircase 3.

   ___ ✓ ___

3. *Objective:* Support a candidate of your choice in his or her campaign for election to a public office.

   Criterion Item: Prove that you have supported a candidate of your choice in his or her campaign for election to a public office.

   ___ ___ ✓

1. No match. Describing a procedure is not the same as carrying out a procedure. The item should provide learners with cash, checks, and deposit slip, and ask them to carry out the verification procedure.

2. No match. Inspecting a staircase is not the same as constructing one. If you want to know if students can construct a staircase, then you must ask each of them to construct one. There is no other way to determine whether they can do it. If it is impractical or impossible to have them do it, have them do the next best thing, perhaps build models of a staircase, and then *infer* whether students have achieved the objective. But remember that you are taking risks in making inferences and that such risks are greater where the consequence of not achieving the objective is larger. (Your students may be able to build models of a staircase, but may not be able to build one actual size that meets safety specifications.)

3. Can't tell. Neither the objective nor the test item describes a performance. What is someone doing when supporting a candidate? Propping the person up? Contributing to the campaign fund? Speaking in the candidate's favor? Unless you know the performances that define *supporting,* you can't decide how to test the objective.

4. *Objective:* Be able to ⟨carry out the⟩ ⟨booking procedure⟩ for an adult violator of any section of the Penal Code that requires taking the subject into custody.

   Criterion Item: George Spelvin, age 23, male, has been caught in the act of setting fire to an office building (Section 448a, PC). ⟨Complete all the steps⟩ needed to book the subject.   ✓ ___ ___

5. *Objective:* Embark on a life-long search for truth, with the willingness and ability to pose questions, examine experience, and construct explanations and meanings.

   Criterion Item: Read *Wisdom from the Mountain* and describe its meaning to you in relation to your life goals.   ___ ___ ✓

6. *Objective:* Be able to ⟨identify and⟩ ⟨mark circuit design errors⟩ on circuit diagrams of transistor amplifiers.

   Criterion Item: Envelope B contains two circuit diagrams of transistor amplifiers. These diagrams contain errors consisting of either missing components, extra components, or components connected in wrong places. ⟨Draw⟩ ⟨a circle⟩ around each error you find.   ✓ ___ ___

4. A match. The objective wants trainees to be able to carry out the booking procedure, and that's what the item asks them to do. The item is appropriate for finding out if the objective has been achieved. Will one item be enough? Should several similar items be used? This, and similar issues, will be discussed in Chapter 6.

5. Can't tell. I'm embarrassed to present you with such statements, but believe it or not, this is an actual "alleged" objective borrowed from a real school. This statement reminds me of the words written above the entrance to a university I attended: "So enter that daily ye may grow in knowledge, wisdom, and love." A beautiful and inspiring sentiment, but hardly an instructional objective.

6. A match. The main intent of the objective is for students to be able to identify circuit design errors. Though it *says* "identify and mark," it seems clear that marking is the indicator that will be used to determine whether learners can identify errors. (If it doesn't seem clear to *you*, then the objective needs revision.) The test item asks students to *circle* errors. Circling is a form of marking, of course, but the more important question is whether circling as an indicator is simple, direct, and well within the repertoire of the student. It meets that criterion, so the item and objective match in performance. (I was once faced with an objective like this, and when tested was asked to *correct* errors on diagrams. When another student asked the instructor about the apparent discrepancy between objective

(Continued on next page.)

6. *(Continued.)*

and test, the reply was, "Well, what good is it to be able to locate an error if you can't correct it? You're not going to go around in life drawing circles around errors, you're going to have to fix them." A seemingly sound argument. So sound, in fact, one might have rebutted—except for fear of reprisal—with the reply that the objective might well have described correcting errors instead.)

5 | Matching the Conditions

Suppose you are working toward the objective of being able to write capital letters, the shape of which conforms to a specified size standard. You practice diligently on all the scratch paper you can find, and begin to feel pretty confident. Then, when exam time comes around, you are handed the following test item.

Write the letters of the alphabet in capital letters. Write them on the slab of butter placed beneath 6 inches of water in the bottom of Sink 3. Write with the wooden stylus provided.

The ensuing conversation with the instructor is imagined to be something like this:

"Wait aminnnit. The objective said I need to be able to write capital letters."

"Correct. And that's precisely what the test item asks you to do."

"But it says I gotta do it on a slab of butter under water!"

"Of course. Anybody can write letters on *paper*. You don't *really* understand how to do it unless you can do it under water. That's the *real* test."

"But the objective didn't say anything about water."

"It doesn't have to. It's obvious that I should be allowed to ask you to write on any surface I decide to. Besides, I'm testing for transfer."

Having somehow survived that ordeal, you now register for a course in TV repair. During this course you are expected to accomplish the following objective:

71

With all parts, tools, and diagrams available, be able to assemble any antenna found in the 1993 Black and Taylor catalog.

And, after properly shredding your fingertips during your practice periods, you are finally ready for the test. When you arrive that day, you are given a piece of paper that says:

On the lab table you will find a package labeled A, containing the parts and diagram needed to assemble a common TV antenna. Using any tools of your choice, assemble the antenna on the roof of the shop garage and mount it on the 50-foot tower.

The ensuing discussion might go something like this:

"Now, see here, kind sir, this test item appears not to be consistent with the objective."

"Oh?"

"Yes, indeed. It appears that the objective tells me to be able to assemble an antenna . . ."

"And that's exactly what the test item asks you to do."

"Please, sir, but I beg to differ. The item says I must do the assembling on the roof of the garage which, as we all know, slopes."

"So?"

"Well, sir, I did all my assembly practice on the floor of the shop. Quite different conditions, you know."

"Oh? Do you think you're going to have a nice level shop floor handy every time you want to put an antenna together?"

"Of course not, sir . . ."

"Well, then, what're you complaining about?"

"Simply that I was not apprised of the conditions under which I would be ultimately expected to perform. Unless you tell me what you, as the expert, think I should be able to do, how will I know what to practice?"

"How could you get this far in the course without knowing that you put antennas together on roofs and not on shop floors?"

"Easily, sir."

"Oh, how?"

"I just believed what I read in the objectives you gave me."

The conditions called for in the test item were different from those called for in the objectives. And readers of this scenario must admire your restraint in not mentioning to the instructor that the test item actually asked for another skill in addition to the one stated in the objective. The objective asked you to *assemble* and the item to *assemble and mount*.

Though these examples may seem rather bizarre (they were chosen for that purpose), you will probably remember even stranger ones as you think back over your years as a student— if you ever saw an objective at all.

So far, you have seen that if you are going to find out whether students have achieved an objective, your test items must ask them to perform what the objective asks them to perform. The point of this chapter is that, in addition, the item must ask students to perform under the same conditions that the objective asks them to perform. If it doesn't, you may learn that students can do *something,* but you will not learn whether they have achieved the objective. If, for example, you want to find out whether students of surgery can tie knots on a slippery gut, you can't find it out if you ask them to tie knots only in string on the back of a chair. If you want to know if students can make change in the presence of harried customers, you will never find it out if you ask them to make change only in a quiet classroom.

Thus, the conditions under which testing is performed should be the same as those called for in the objective.

If the conditions are not the same in both test item and objective, you will not know whether the objective has been achieved. And if you do not find out whether your objectives (which you say are important) are achieved, then you will not know how effective your instruction has been or what to do to make it better.

In practice, there are two common ways in which an item that appears to match an objective in performance may still be *inappropriate:*

1. The item asks for the performance under more, or less, stringent conditions than called for by the objective.
2. The item asks for more skills than called for by the objective.

Often you will encounter both deficiencies in the same test item (as illustrated by the TV antenna caper).

MATCHING CONDITIONS

The rule is simple: *Make the test items include the same conditions (no more, no less) as are included in the objective.* And the reason is simple—that's the way you will find out if the objective has been achieved.

Here are a few practice items.

Below are pairs of statements, each consisting of an objective and a potential test item. The performances look like they match, but the conditions may or may not match. Check (√) the appropriate column to the right, depending on whether conditions in the item match conditions in the objective.

Do the conditions match?

YES   NO

1. *Objective:* Be able to introduce yourself to a peer in a suitable manner (i.e., look the person in the face, offer a firm handshake, give your name, repeat his or her name when it is given, express pleasure at making his or her acquaintance).

   Criterion Item: The instructor will point to various members of the class. Introduce yourself to them in a suitable manner.   ___ ___

2. *Objective:* Given a well-stated objective, be able to prepare a criterion test suitable for assessing achievement of the objective.

   Criterion Item: Prepare a criterion test for the following objective:
   At end of the course, the student will find learning to be an exciting adventure, choosing to participate fully and independently.   ___ ___

3. *Objective:* Given a person with a first-degree burn on any part of his or her body, be able to apply first aid using the steps outlined in the Red Cross manual for treatment of first-degree burns.

   Criterion Item: Instructor points to patient lying on table with midsection exposed, and says, "This patient has a first-degree burn on her posterior. Treat it according to the Red Cross manual."   ___ ___

Turn the page to check your responses.

1. *Objective:* Be able to introduce yourself to a peer in a suitable manner (i.e., look the person in the face, offer a firm handshake, give your name, repeat his or her name when it is given, express pleasure at making his or her acquaintance).

   Criterion Item: The instructor will point to various members of the class. Introduce yourself to them in a suitable manner.

   ✓   ___

2. *Objective:* Given a well-stated objective, be able to prepare a criterion test suitable for assessing achievement of the objective.

   Criterion Item: Prepare a criterion test for the following objective:
   At end of the course, the student will find learning to be an exciting adventure, choosing to participate fully and independently.

   ___   ✓

3. *Objective:* Given a person with a first-degree burn on any part of his or her body, be able to apply first aid using the steps outlined in the Red Cross manual for treatment of first-degree burns.

   Criterion Item: Instructor points to patient lying on table with midsection exposed, and says, "This patient has a first-degree burn on her posterior. Treat it according to the Red Cross manual."

   ✓   ___

76

1. A match. The performances match—both test item and objective ask the student to exhibit the same performance. And the conditions? Well, the objective just says the student is expected to be able to introduce himself or herself to peers. It doesn't specify any special or unusual conditions within which the introducing is to occur. The test item asks for the performance in a classroom. That is acceptable, inasmuch as there is nothing in the objective to suggest otherwise. Had the objective asked for the performance in "social situations" or for introductions to "strangers," I would consider the test item a simulation or approximation from which achievement of the objective would have to be inferred.

2. No match. Both the test and the objective ask the student to prepare a criterion test. So far, so good. But the objective asks that the student be able to prepare a test that fits a well-stated objective. The "objective" stated in the test item not only is not well stated, it isn't any sort of objective at all. It may be a lovely sentence for a public relations department to use in promoting a school, but it is not an objective. Thus, the conditions do not match.

3. A match. Both objective and test item ask for application of first aid to a person with a first-degree burn. The question of how many items of this type may be needed to adequately test for competence will be discussed a little later.

Try three more practice items on page 79.

Practice Items

4. *Objective:* Given any model of Disaster Master aircraft, be able to remove and replace any engine part.

   Criterion Item: On Table 3 are engines from three different Disaster Master aircraft, and a new engine part for each. For each engine, remove the old part and replace it with the new.   ___ ___

5. *Objective:* For a blouse made of any material, be able to repair bad stitches or skipped stitches.

   Criterion Item: Inspect the pile of clothing on Table 4 and repair any incorrect work.   ___ ___

6. *Objective:* After hearing any pair of single-syllable words spoken by the instructor, state whether the words rhyme.

   Criterion Item: On the following page are pairs of words that have only one syllable. Put a check beside the pairs of words that rhyme.   ___ ___

Turn the page to check your responses.

79

4. *Objective:* Given any model of Disaster Master aircraft, be able to remove and replace any engine part.

   Criterion Item: On Table 3 are engines from three different Disaster Master aircraft, and a new engine part for each. For each engine, remove the old part and replace it with the new. ___ ✓

5. *Objective:* For a blouse made of any material, be able to repair bad stitches or skipped stitches.

   Criterion Item: Inspect the pile of clothing on Table 4 and repair any incorrect work. ___ ✓

6. *Objective:* After hearing any pair of single-syllable words spoken by the instructor, state whether the words rhyme.

   Criterion Item: On the following page are pairs of words that have only one syllable. Put a check beside the pairs of words that rhyme. ___ ✓

4. No match. The objective says the student needs to be able to do something to an *airplane*; specifically, to take out and replace engine parts. The item asks the student to take out and replace parts in engines that are sitting on *a table*. If you have ever looked under the hood of a car or tried to work on an installed car engine, you can well imagine that it is one thing to work on an engine in a car and quite another to do something to an engine sitting on a table. So the performances match but the conditions don't.

5. No match. There are two problems with this pair of statements. First, though both objective and test item ask the student to be able to repair, the objective expects to see the skill of "repairing bad or skipped stitches," while the test item asks to see the skill of "repairing any incorrect work." Thus, though both use the word "repair"—and thereby lull us into thinking the performances match—the test item is asking for more skill than the objective.

   Second, the conditions don't match. The objective wants the student to be able to apply his or her skill to blouses, the test item to unspecified types of clothing. You may think the difference trivial, but only if you've never been faced with test items that ask for something different from what you were led to expect.

6. No match. The main intent of both objective and test item is the discrimination of rhyming sounds. But the objective says the student will *hear* words and tell if they rhyme, and the item says he or she will have to *read* words and tell if they rhyme. Hearing isn't the same as reading, so the stimuli to which the student is expected to respond do not match.

   Would you rather say that the performances are different, that responding to auditory stimuli is different from responding to visual stimuli? All right. As long as

(Continued on next page.)

6. *(Continued.)*

you conclude that there is no match it doesn't much matter what labels you put on the parts.

APPROXIMATIONS

Sometimes the *match the conditions in the items with the conditions in the objective* rule must be bent and, occasionally, twisted literally out of shape.

Consider this objective, from a course on how to repair atomic bombs at Hypothetical U (now known as Crater Lake II).

> *When faced with a malfunctioning atomic bomb of 10 kiloton or less, and when shown one symptom, be able to repair the malfunction. Repair must be completed within 45 minutes. The repaired weapon is to function within manufacturer's specifications.*

As you must guess, it might be somewhat impractical to create a test in which the student is given a live malfunctioning bomb. Making the conditions on the test match the conditions of the objective might be somewhat foolhardy. The consequence of an error is just potentially too great to warrant following the rule. After all, this doesn't seem to be a situation in which a serious error is likely to be followed by little more than an embarrassed "Oooops."

It's clear what the objective wants. It wants students to be able to fix troubles. So far so good. And to find out if students can fix troubles, you must ask them to fix troubles. That's clear, too. But in this case it's too dangerous to let them demonstrate their skill on the real thing. What can you do?

You can simulate. You can approximate. You can give the students some sort of pretend bomb and ask them do what the objective wants them to be able to do. If they can do it with the pretend bomb, you will have to assume they can do it with the real thing. Is that a safe assumption? Depends on how closely your conditions match those of the objective. If you only have to approximate *one* condition, your guess as to whether they will be able to perform under the real conditions will be better than if you have to approximate two or more conditions. If, for example, bomb repair is done under stressful conditions and you watch students repair in the calm of the classroom, you would be less confident of their ability to do it "out there" than if you had provided some real stress during the performance on the pretend bomb.

Two points. First, *never* simulate performance. Always ask your students to *do* that which the objective asks them to do, even though you must provide simulated conditions. Second, remember that when you simulate or approximate conditions, you have to make *inferences* about whether students will be able to do the "real thing" asked for by the objective. You will have to make an educated guess about whether the objective has been achieved, after watching performance under less-than-ideal conditions.

Sometimes we can provide conditions *close* to those called for by the objective, and sometimes the conditions will be considerably different from those called for by the objective.

Suppose, for another example, that the objective says something like

Be able to rescue a drowning person.

If you want to find out if the objective is achieved, it's pretty clear that you will have to simulate the conditions. I suppose you and your students could hang around the beaches waiting for the right moment, but that would be inefficient. Fun, perhaps, but inefficient. So some approximation would have to do. What kind of approximation? The closest approximation to the real thing that you can arrange. Rather than ask students to answer multiple-choice questions on the history of drowning, or have them describe how they would save an unfortunate drowning person, provide them with someone who is pretending to need help and ask each student to perform the desired skills. That is, wherever possible, ask students to perform the *main intent,* even though the conditions under which it is exhibited are somewhat different from those that represent the real thing.

Consider the poor professor of medicine who wants to know if his students can perform an appendectomy. He can't just run down to the street and snag a number of people with "Hi there. Mind having your appendix out?" If he doesn't have enough patients to go around, he must do some approximating. As one alternative, he could find out if students can perform each of the subskills separately. That is, he could find out if each student knew where to make an incision, how to retract, how to tie off, and so on. But while that would tell him whether subordinate objectives were achieved, it would not tell him if students could perform the meaningful skill of performing an appendectomy. It would not qualify as a simulation or an approximation, because the skill called for in the item is not the same as that called for in the objective. *Unless performances match, you can't conclude you are approximating.* So what can the professor do? Well, he could use one of the mannequins that have been created for use in surgery simulations, asking each student to remove the appendix of the mannequin. Learners are performing the desired skill, of course, but under conditions rather different from those faced with a live patient.

He could also ask each student to remove the appendix from a cadaver. Here again learners would be performing the relevant skill, but again under conditions different from those faced with live patients. But knowing that he must simulate, he arranges a situation that is as much like the real thing (conditions stated in the objective) as possible. And then, after observing the performance of students in the simulation situation, the professor *infers* what each student will be able to do in the objective-defined situation. He hasn't observed students performing the objective, so he doesn't *know* they can perform as desired. He *infers* whether or not students can perform as desired by watching them perform under approximated conditions.

When it is a small approximation—that is, when conditions are very close to those called for in the objective—it is a small inference, a small leap. For instance, if the objective says

Be able to select (collect) *from the storeroom those instruments and equipment needed to perform an appendectomy,*

and if the item says

On your answer sheet write the number of the instruments and equipment used in the performance of an appendectomy. An array of numbered equipment and instruments are located on Table 5,

the performances match but the conditions don't. Selecting tools from a table is not the same as selecting them from a storeroom. The difference is so small, however, that you aren't taking much of a risk in using this type of item. That is, if students can select tools from a table, it is a pretty small risk to assume they can select them from a storeroom. The inference is a small one.

Suppose the test item said

On the following page are sketches of a variety of surgical instruments and equipment. Check those that are used in the performance of an appendectomy.

Again, the performances match (both objective and item ask learners to select instruments from "givens"), but the conditions don't. The objective says select from a storeroom, and the item says select from sketches. The inference is larger. The hope is that if students can recognize sketches on paper, they can also recognize the real thing in a storeroom. But the leap from sketches on paper to instruments in storeroom is larger than the leap from instruments on table to instruments in storeroom. Why? Because sketches of instruments are not the same as the instruments themselves. Sketches are only representations of that which students are expected to recognize. Thus, as the things given students are *less* like the things described in the objective, the simulation increases. As the simulation increases, the size of the inference increases. Perhaps I can clarify this point with Figure 3. On the far left of the figure is the performance called for by the objective. If a test item asks for that performance directly, under the conditions described

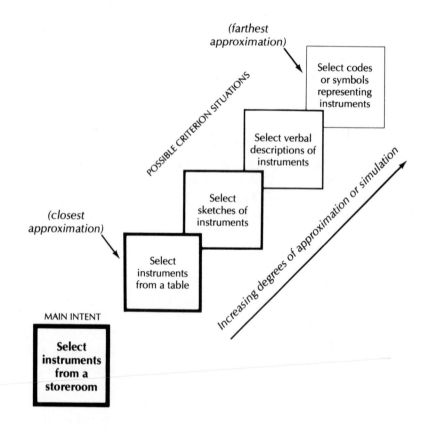

Figure 3.   *As approximation of the main intent increases, inference increases.*

in the objective, there is no simulation or approximation, and one can decide directly whether the objective has been achieved. The boxes behind the left-hand box show situations progressively *less* like that called for by the objective. Selecting instruments from a table is a little less like selecting them from a storeroom; selecting sketches of instruments is still less direct than selecting the real thing; selecting verbal descriptions of instruments is considerably different from selecting the real thing; selecting codes or symbols of the real thing (such as a verbal description written in Morse code) is about as far from the intention of the objective as I can imagine. The farther one moves to the right in Figure 3, the greater the difference between *observed* performance and *intended* performance, and the greater the difference between the thing actually identified and the thing intended to be identified (as described by the objective). Thus, the farther one moves to the right, the greater the inference from the performance you *see* to the performance you *want* as the intended objective.

How large an inference can you tolerate? *It depends on the consequence of an error.* If the consequence of *not* performing as desired is tolerable, then a larger inference is tolerable. If the consequence of not performing as desired is *serious,* then a large inference (large difference between conditions in item and objective) is dangerous and should not be tolerated.

In the present example, the consequence of not being able to perform an appendectomy properly can be as large as the loss of a patient. While such a loss is not nearly as great as the consequence of a commercial pilot's inability to land a planeload of passengers properly, the loss of a life is always considered a serious consequence. When the potential consequence can be this large, it is important to have students demonstrate their achievement of the objective before certifying them to perform on their own.

If the objective describes an ability to add, on the other hand, what is the consequence of an error? If it is only that a little time will be lost, or that inappropriate change will be made, a larger inference is tolerable.

So whenever you are unable to make the conditions in the test item match the conditions in the objective, try to follow this rule:

Make the inference as small as possible by making the test item conditions approximate objective conditions as closely as possible.

How large or tenuous an inference is tolerable? I don't know. You'll have to judge for yourself. Judge the consequence of not achieving the objective by answering such questions as: "If some students cannot perform the objective when they leave my instruction, they are likely to _____." The answer should help you decide how much energy to put into finding out whether the objective is achieved as written.

DODGE CITY

Some people use some strange dodges or arguments to justify use of items that don't match the objectives. It doesn't seem to matter that by doing so they prevent themselves from finding out whether their objectives are achieved. Some of these arguments go like this:

"But I like my tests to be interesting."

Or, "I like to use a *variety* of items on my tests."

Or, "Why, that's just teaching the test."

Or, "Well, sure the objective says learners need to be able to DO it, but they don't really understand it unless they can _____" (define it, describe it, tell the history of it, write an essay on it, teach it).

My reply to these attempts to avoid the issue is simple and persistent: *If the items don't match the objective you won't know if the objective has been achieved.* Make your test as interesting as you want, but not at the expense of items that fit.

WHAT'S YOUR PLEASURE?

You have now practiced all the pieces of the skill of matching test items to objectives; that is, you have practiced all the subordinate skills. All that remains is to practice the entire skill. So you will now have the option of some guided practice to put it all together.

But there are two other options I'd like to offer at this point. Though the purpose of the book is to consider only the issue of how to recognize criterion items relevant to assessing achievement of an objective, there are some related questions buzzing around, such as the number and range of items to use for a test. Though I may not answer the one(s) distressing you the most, I'd like to try my hand at three or four of them. So one option is to go on to Chapter 6, Peripheralia.

The other option is to go directly to the criterion test in Chapter 8, Got a Match?, instead of to the guided practice in Chapter 7. It's up to you. What's your pleasure?

Peripheralia (odds and ends)   **page 91**

A Pride of Items (guided practice)   **page 105**

Got a Match? (criterion test)   **page 135**

6 ‖ Peripheralia

No matter how I try to confine myself to a specific topic (in the present case the selection of test items relevant to an objective), there are always loose ends. There are always some more or less related issues and questions raised by those who help in shaping-up a book. The problem is similar to that of trying to explain in detail the workings of some part of the body. Invariably there are questions about how a particular part connects to, interacts with, and influences the functioning of other parts. Though I would like to simply fold up my typewriter at this point and send you off into the exciting practice chapter, I must first deal with a few pieces of peripheralia—oddments that have something to do with testing. They may be terribly important issues, but they are not strictly related to the skill of being able to recognize items that are appropriate to objectives.

HOW MANY ITEMS?

A question that often arises when trying to determine whether an objective has been achieved is "How many items should I use?"

"Why, it depends on the objective," is always the first answer that plops out.

"You don't say," you reply with a properly hurt tone, ready to run out the door. "Must you talk in fuzzies?"[1]

Well, no. The question of the number of items truly is one that should be considered, even though it is not relevant to the

---

1. For a full description of *fuzzies,* see Chapter 3 of *Goal Analysis, Second Edition,* R. F. Mager (David S. Lake Publishers, 1984).

achievement of the objective stated for this book. The answer is based mainly on two things:

The range of stimulus conditions described or implied by the objective.

The criterion of acceptable performance stated in the objective.

Overt Main Intent.   Let's consider the easiest case first, where the performance mentioned in the objective is both *overt* and the *main intent* (see Figure 4 below). In this case there is only *one type* or one form of item that is appropriate—the type that asks students to do what the objective says they must do. Consider again the objective about riding a unicycle:

Be able to ride a unicycle 100 yards on a paved level surface without falling off.

It is clear that the only way we can find out if the objective is achieved is to ask each student to ride.

Suppose a few students get on their trusty one-wheelers and wobble all the way down to the end of the block, wavering

Figure 4

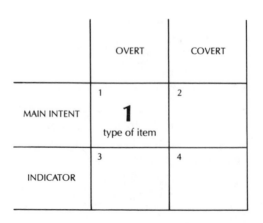

some but not falling. Would you agree they have achieved the objective? If so, that's the end of it. You wanted to know if they could ride, they rode, and you certify that they have achieved that objective.

But suppose you say, "Maybe these students just rode that far by sheer luck. I wouldn't be willing to say they've achieved the objective unless they can ride 100 yards two times in a row." In such a case you would be using two test items to determine achievement of a single objective. That would be all right, provided that each and every item matches the objective in performance and conditions. Instead of twice in a row, you might feel that two rides out of three tries would be needed for you to be willing to certify these students. All right, so long as each and every item matches the objective in performance and conditions. (It would also be proper to add to the objective the criterion you intend to use.)

Stimulus Range. Now I want to split a hair with you. The objective we have been considering says "Be able to ride *a* unicycle. . . ." This means that it doesn't matter *which* unicycle each student rides during his or her test. As long as it is a unicycle you will have to accept that. That's what the objective says. But if the objective said "Be able to ride *any* unicycle . . . ," we would have a spoke of a different color. In this case it is pretty clear that a single test item wouldn't satisfy you. That is, it is unlikely that you would be willing to agree that students could ride *any* unicycle if you only see each one riding *one* unicycle. Which brings us to the type of objective that calls for a performance to be exhibited with a *range* of stimulus conditions. *Any objective falls into this class if the student is expected to use the same things under different conditions, or different things under the same or different conditions, when exhibiting the performance expected.*

Let me try that again. If students are expected to manipulate different things while doing what the objective wants them to do, then you would want to use as many test items as needed to sample the *range* of things to be manipulated. Thus, if the objective said it wanted students to be able to solve problems of a certain type, you would use as many test items as needed to sample the problems the objective is talking about. Of course, *each and every item* must ask students to solve that specific kind of problem: each and every item must match the objective.

If, on the other hand, the objective said it wanted students to be able to exhibit their performance under a variety of conditions, you would use as many items as needed to sample the *range* of relevant conditions. For example, if an objective wanted a student pilot to land a plane on *any* serviceable airstrip, you would ask each student to make as many landings as it would take to sample the *range* of serviceable airstrips. If students were expected to make those landings in a variety of weather conditions, items would be needed that asked for landings on a variety of strips in a variety of weather conditions. In this case each student would be using (manipulating) the same thing (an airplane) during each item, but the conditions of use would be different.

Thus, the answer to the question of how many items to use is this: Use as many items as are needed to sample the range of givens (i.e., the things students will have to work with) and the range of conditions. But make certain that each and every item used matches the objective.

Here is an example of an objective that asks students to be able to perform with a range of stimuli (givens).

> *Given all pertinent facts and figures, prepare* (fill in) *federal tax Form 1040 (personal income tax), following all instructions that accompany the federal form and in accordance with all existing federal tax laws.*

In this example it is clear that there is not just *one* set of facts and figures students are to be able to deal with, but any number of such sets. To find out whether students have achieved the objective, then, one would want to give them several sets of facts and figures and ask them to do their stuff.

How many test items would you need? As many as would sample the range of facts and figures each student is likely to run into. I don't know how many that is. If you are a subject matter expert in tax work, though, *you* would know how many items they would have to complete in order for you to say with confidence that they have achieved the objective. But of course each and every item would have to give students facts and figures and ask them to fill out Form 1040.

Here is an example of an objective that contains a single given and a range of conditions.

> *Given a soldering gun, solder, and flux, be able to replace any given component in the Model 10 Brainwasher.*

In this case students are using the same tool no matter which component they are replacing. But there are undoubtedly differences in the conditions under which the replacement must be accomplished. If you have never seen the Model 10 Brainwasher, I can assure you that some components need to be replaced under tightly confined conditions (in tight spaces), and some components need to be replaced while the replacer is almost standing on his or her head. So to find out if the objective is achieved, you would need to ask students to replace components in as many parts of the machine as are needed to represent the range of conditions under which the replacement is expected to be done.

When thinking of variations in space and confinement conditions, one immediately thinks of the plight of the plumber and of the auto mechanic. When you look at the conditions under which they must replace an elbow and adjust a carburetor, it makes you wonder if they have to pass some sort of contortionist test before being allowed into the clan.

To summarize the issue pertaining to the number of test items needed to assess achievement of any objective:

1. Use as many test items as are needed to sample the range of stimuli (givens) and/or conditions.
2. Make certain that each item matches the objective.

There is a final comment that I hesitate to make because of its obviousness—a third test of the adequacy of a series of test items, in addition to the ones listed above. No matter how many items you have prepared or selected, no matter how pretty they are, if *you* will not be willing to certify each student who performs well on those items as having accomplished the objective, there is something wrong either with your objective or your items. It's no good to put yourself into the bind of "Even if students perform on these five items, I still wouldn't be willing to say they've achieved the objective." If that's your feeling, your item testing isn't finished, regardless of what the items look like. But if the items meet the first two tests and you still feel you wouldn't certify students who perform on them, it would be in order for you to reexamine your feeling. How do you do that? In this case, you take another look at the objective, because the trouble is likely to be there. The trouble is probably that the objective doesn't accurately describe what it is you want students to be able to do. If there is something *more* you want students to do than is expressed by your items, it is likely that the objective needs revision.

The Rule of Reason.   While we're on the subject of "how many items make a test" it would be well to mention the rule of reason relating to item range. It is terribly tempting to create bizarre or improbable items when an objective describes a range of givens or conditions. "Oh, well," the argument often goes, "they don't *really* understand those problems unless they can solve them while being strung up by their toes," or "they can't *really* be said to know how to diagnose illness unless they can recognize symptoms of Martian malady and Diddle-finger's disease." Sometimes items calling for performance with highly improbable givens are created solely to keep the instructor amused. After all, it can get rather boring to test students over and over again with items that are reasonable and practical. But the result of all this is that the instructor still doesn't find out if the objective is achieved, still doesn't find out how well students are likely to do that which is to be expected of them.

In this case the rule of reason says:

When a range of stimuli and/or conditions is to be used in a series of test items, use *only* those stimuli and conditions that students will encounter within approximately six months of the time they are tested.

This rule means simply that the items should match the objective in performance, and that the givens and conditions should be reasonable. What's reasonable? Well, it's reasonable to prepare students to handle situations they will run into within the immediate future. It is not reasonable to insist that they be able to handle situations that are known to be highly improbable. There is nothing magical about the six months; it is merely a guide. If in your situation three or nine months makes more sense, then that is the guide to use. If you are an expert in your subject, you will either know what is probable and not probable, or you can find out. If you can't find out, then don't write test items.

If it is important that students be able to handle a situation that may occur only rarely, and if the consequence is dire (e.g., "If the red light ever goes on, fer crissakes push the panic button"), then give them refresher training often enough to warrant confidence that the skill will be there if needed.

GRADING

Another question that often oozes to the surface has to do with that weird practice called grading. The issue shows itself in a variety of forms.

"But if all the students get it right, how can I give grades?"

"If the items are too easy, everybody will get them right."

"Gee, I'm not allowed to give everybody an A, no matter how well they can perform. It just isn't done."

"What about the students who try hard but don't quite make the criterion? Surely you don't expect me to fail them?"

"What about the students who do ten times more than I ask for—surely I can't give them the same grade as the ones who just barely squeak through?"

Each of these sentiments arises from a concern caused by the shift from the old norm-referenced way of grading to the criterion-referenced method of grading. In the old days it seemed appropriate to grade students by comparing them with each other. It didn't seem to matter whether the best students could do what instructors wanted them to be able to do; if they were better at something than anyone else in the class, they got the highest grade.

But look at this flight-plight of a best-in-class performance. Imagine you are flying along in a jumbo jet when the pilot comes on the intercom to say, "Ladies and gentlemen, we are about to begin our descent. There is absolutely nothing to worry about." And then adds, condescendingly, "I got perfect scores on almost all my exams . . . I only flunked landing." The norm-referenced system is simply not appropriate when you have important objectives for students to achieve. You don't care how hard certain students tried, you don't care how close they got, if they *can't* perform they mustn't be certified as being *able* to perform. You want to know *why* a student failed to achieve an objective, of course, so you can help him or her to mastery. But until that student can perform, he or she must not be certified as being able to perform.

If you have objectives that are important to achieve—that is, if there is a genuine need for them to be achieved because a meaningful consequence would result in achievement or non-achievement—then it is also important that you find out if that achievement was accomplished. You cannot do so by comparing one student with another. You can only do so by comparing the performance of each student with the performance called for by the objective.

And if, when that comparison is made, you find that some students can perform as desired, should they not be certified as being able to perform as desired? And what if other students *cannot* perform as desired? Should some of them be certified

merely because their non-performance is better than the non-performance of anyone else in the class? How nutty can we get?

"Oh, but I couldn't give everybody an A," is a comment often heard. But why not? If an A means that a student is able to perform each of the objectives, why would you not be willing to certify that he or she can perform? What does it mean to say you are "not allowed to give everybody an A"? If it means that your institution or school system isn't designed to cope with that much success, then some serious changes are in order. If it means that there would be adverse consequences to you because too many of your students were successful, then some serious changes are in order. Whenever the normal curve is used as a basis for grading, the user is legislating *in advance* the amount of success he or she will tolerate. With the curve system one is saying to the students, "It doesn't matter how well you can perform . . . only a certain percentage of you will be allowed to think of yourselves as totally successful."

Some schools have given up the norm-referenced grading system and have gone to a pass-fail arrangement. But what does *pass* mean? Nobody knows. In some courses it means that a minimum score on an exam has been made. In others, that attendance was adequate. In still others it means that students have completed all the assignments set out for them. But pass is little better than a grade unless the nature and the number of the objectives that are represented by the pass or the grade are made public. A more meaningful reporting system is one that identifies the competencies accomplished by individual students; this way one knows what specific students are able to do, instead of merely knowing that they are considered passable or that they are more or less competent than their chance peers.

ITEM DIFFICULTY

It has been common practice to try to arrange the difficulty of a test item so that just about half the students get it right. Difficulty indices are often computed for each item, on the grounds that an item must not be too easy or too hard.

This is a norm-referenced practice, and it has nothing to do with the practice of finding out if objectives have been achieved. The practice is perfectly defensible when one wants to know how well a given student can perform in relation to his or her peers, or when testing the *extent* of someone's content knowledge in a given area. But if you want to know whether people can do something you want them to do, what's the sense of being arbitrarily devious by making items easier or harder? Ask them simply and directly to do the thing you are after.

The expression "the item was too easy" implies a terrible thing about the nature of education. It implies that rather than work to help as many students as possible to achieve important objectives, many educators are instead going to *limit* the amount of instructional success they will tolerate. It implies that if too many students are able to perform as desired, rather than jump up and down with joy at such success, many educators will arbitrarily make the test more difficult.

Unfortunately, there is substance to these implications. Education is *not* yet designed to be totally successful; many educators *do* limit the amount of success they will allow. As mentioned earlier, the use of the normal curve is evidence of such limitation. No matter how well the students perform, no matter how many meet or exceed the instructor's expectations, only a portion of them will be allowed to think of themselves as competent. Conversely, no matter how poorly a group of students performs, those who perform the best will be given a label (grade) signifying success.

There is further evidence to support the allegation that education is not designed to tolerate total success. Ask yourself and your colleagues what would happen to them if their instruction *were* totally successful, and that as a result they gave every student an A and could prove the grades were deserved. Would this result in a banquet in their honor? Applause from their peers? A raise from the administration? Seldom. Though there are now a few institutions that will tolerate total instructional success, the majority still seem bent on fulfilling the prophecy of the normal curve. And that, I feel, is more than unprofessional; it borders on fraud.

Don't worry about item difficulty. Make it clear and make it match the objective. If everyone performs perfectly, shout with joy. Or with Mary, if you prefer. But in any case, rejoice.

AFFECTIVE OBJECTIVES

You may have noticed that all the examples used so far have dealt with performances in the knowing and doing categories. Nothing whatever has been said about *affective* objectives. This is not an oversight, I assure you. And, though it is perfectly clear to me why they haven't been mentioned, I'm not sure I can make it clear to you. But I'll try.

There is no question that such issues as attitudes, motivation, growth, and development are of great importance. You do indeed concern yourselves with how students feel about the instruction you give them, you do indeed care about their values and their aspirations. But all these words describe *abstract* states or conditions, and the only way you can make inferences about the existence or shape of such states is through what someone says or what someone does—in other words, through overt performances or indicator behaviors. And if you have statements describing desired student performances, you can call those statements objectives. And if you have objectives, you ought to be able to match criterion items or situations that will tell you if the objectives have been achieved. The procedure described in this book should provide a guide to that end.

Notice I haven't referred to those objectives as "affective objectives." I see no need to do that; besides, most of the statements called affective objectives are, in my opinion, mislabeled. They ought to be called goals. Though they mention intended achievement of some sort of abstract state, they do not identify the performances that define that state, that would tell you if the state exists as intended.

With these comments I am not sluffing off the importance of feelings and attitudes; to the contrary, I am convinced that attention to feelings and attitudes is more important than much of the subject matter occupying instructors' attention.

But to say that feelings and attitudes are important is one thing; to say that *therefore* there are such things as "affective objectives" is quite another.

If this issue is one of concern to you, or if I haven't satisfied your feeling that I am treating the issue too casually, I'd like to refer you to two small books that address themselves specifically to this topic.[2]

WHAT NEXT?

The next chapter offers some guided practice in applying all the steps associated with matching items to objectives, starting with a complete example to show how you might apply each of the steps in the matching procedure. If you don't feel the need for more practice, however, you should go directly to the criterion test at the end of the book. You decide.

I'd like to practice the entire skill   **page 105**

I'm ready to test my skill   **page 135**

---

2. Read *Developing Attitude Toward Learning, Second Edition,* R. F. Mager (David S. Lake Publishers, 1984) and *Goal Analysis, Second Edition,* R. F. Mager (David S. Lake Publishers, 1984).

7 | A Pride of Items

Before blazing through the criterion test offered on page 135, you may be taking the option offered here to practice the objective-item matching skill in its entirety. One of the most pervasive instructional errors is that of sending students away without having had practice doing that which is the object of the instruction, or having practiced only the parts and not the whole. (A widely practiced variation of this error is that of giving students practice in performing as desired, and then testing at some higher level of discourse than that which was practiced.) Not wishing to be guilty of this common malpractice, I hereby offer optional exercises containing the same kind of items you will find on the criterion test in Chapter 8. (Keep the removable Objective/Item Checklist card handy to remind yourself of the steps. It's located between the last page and the back cover of this book.) Three kinds of practice will be presented, followed by information with which you can check your own responses.

1. *Yes or no.* Each practice item will consist of an objective and a criterion item. Your task will be to say whether the item is appropriate for assessing achievement of the objective. While you might feel that several items would be needed to determine if the objective has been accomplished, you will be asked only to say whether the presented item matches the objective.

2. *Which, if any.* Each practice item will consist of an objective and a series of items, each allegedly appropriate for assessing achievement of the objective. Your task will be to review each item and say whether it is or is not appropriate for testing the objective.

3. *Fix it.* Each practice item will consist of an objective and an allegedly appropriate item. But something will be wrong. Either the objective will need some repair, or for some reason the item won't match. Your task will be to repair things so that the item will be satisfactory as a test of the objective. If you apply the step-by-step procedure for checking the appropriateness of an item (Objective/Item Checklist), you shouldn't have any trouble.

"Wait a minute," I hear you saying. "How come the objective of the book asks me to be able to identify items that match objectives, and now you want me to do a repair job?" And a very astute question that is, as well as being accurate. You are correct; the objective is for you to be able to recognize test items that do or don't match their objective, and that is exactly what you will be asked to do on the criterion test in Chapter 8. By asking you to repair a few objectives and/or items, you are likely to attend more closely to the critical characteristics of each. But the fixing is just for practice; it wouldn't be correct to ask you to fix objectives and items on the criterion test merely because it was "covered" in the instruction. In Chapter 8, you will be tested only with items that match the objective of the book.

WORKING THROUGH THE MATCHING TASK

During testing of an earlier draft of the manuscript, one of the testees suggested that before practicing the entire skill, another example or two of how I work through the matching task would be helpful. So, on the chance that it might be useful, I'll show you an objective and an item and then write down the stream of thought that ekes forth as I work my way through.

Example 1

Objective: Given a group of numerical expressions, be able to circle examples of the commutative property of addition.

Criterion Item: Underline the numerical expressions that are examples of the commutative property of addition.

(a)	$3+7=2+8$	(d)	$5+2=2+5$
(b)	$4+5=5+4$	(e)	$9+1=5+5$
(c)	$0+4=4+0$	(f)	$6+2=2+6$

Thoughts While Matching. What's the performance called for in the objective? "Circle examples" is what it says. I'll circle that so it won't escape. Now what's the main intent? Well, the objective wants students to be able to recognize examples of the commutative property (whatever that is) when they see them. That means circling is an indicator. Is it the simplest, most direct indicator I can think of? Not bad. Circling is easy to do and the quality of the circling is not likely to be confused with the quality of the recognizing. Is circling well within the repertoire of the students? I can't tell for sure unless I know exactly who the target population is. Unless it is a group that does not yet know how to use a pencil, the indicator should be okay.

Now for the item. The item wants students to underline numerical expressions. I'll circle that. Now. Do the performances match? Well, circling isn't exactly the same behavior as underlining, but they both indicate whether students can recognize the desired property, and they are both simple and direct. So the performances match.

What about the conditions? The objective says students are to be given some numerical expressions to work with, and the item does just that. The objective asks them to indicate examples of the commutative property, and the item does, too. So the item matches the objective.

Example 2

Here's an example of the same process when the objective exists and the test item is just being drafted.

Objective: Given common situations of human interactions (either filmed or actual), be able to say whether the consequence to a specified behavior will increase or decrease the likelihood that the behavior will be repeated in the future.

Thoughts While Drafting. What's the performance stated in the objective? *Say.* Quick. Circle it. Is that a main intent or an indicator? Well, it looks like an indicator. Looks as though the main intent is for students to be able to decide *(judge)* whether a given consequence will have a facilitating or inhibiting effect on a given behavior. Is the indicator the simplest possible? Looks okay, provided the student is asked only to say "increase" or "decrease."

Now about the item. Since I want to record students' responses, I'll just ask them to circle one of two words that I will provide near the item, rather than have them write the words. It's simpler. I will need to present students with situations and tell them which behavior and which consequence they should respond to. I'll draft an item.

Draft of Criterion Item: Watch Scene 12 of the film provided, and circle the word below that describes the most likely effect of the consequence.

How's that? Terrible. Sounds good, but it doesn't tell the students what behavior and what consequence to evaluate. I'll try again.

Criterion Item: Watch Scene 12 of the film provided, in which the behavior of the boy is followed by an action (consequence) by the girl. Circle the words below that describe whether the consequence will make it more, or less, likely that the boy will behave that way again.

> *More likely   Less likely*

How's that? Well, better. But do my indicators match? The objective says to be able to tell whether there will be an increase or decrease in the likelihood of a behavior, and my item asks students to tell whether the behavior will be more likely or less likely. Is that the same thing? Yes. Different words, same skill. Okay. All I have to do now is to construct additional items in a similar manner.

You can see that though I appeared not to have followed each of the checklist items in the precise order given, I did ask the relevant questions, I did use the checklist items as a guide. After you've used it a few times, you will be able to get along without it most of the time.

Note: If you are lucky enough to be dealing with an objective that states BOTH the main intent and an indicator, you will have an easier time of preparing or matching items. Just follow the path for an indicator, starting with Step 2 of the checklist.

And now for some practice.

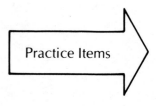

Practice Items

YES OR NO

Below is a series of items, each consisting of an objective and a test item. If the item matches the objective—that is, if the item is suitable for testing achievement of the objective—check (√) the YES column to the right. If the item is not suitable, for whatever reason, check (√) the NO column. (If checking is against your politics, make a mark of your choice. But do something to indicate your decision.)

A match?

YES   NO

1. *Objective:* Given Sunday comics, be able to list all of the individual strip titles within the classifications of dry humor, light humor, romance, mysteries, detective, adventure, sociological, or religious.

   Criterion Item: Check the comic strip that deals with light humor.
(a) Dick Tracy	(c) Mary Worth
(b) Nancy	(d) Little Orphan Annie
   ___ ___

2. *Objective:* Be able to list five major pieces of legislation that were passed in the United States during the Progressive Era (1900–1917).

   Criterion Item: Underline five of the following pieces of twentieth-century legislation that were passed during the Progressive Era (1900–1917).
(a) Pure Food and Drug Act	(d) Hepburn Act
(b) Federal Reserve Act	(e) Prohibition Act
(c) Underwood Tariff	(f) Social Security Act
   ___ ___

3. *Objective:* Given ten minority groups in the United States, list at least eight of them in order according to total population.

   Criterion Item: What are eight of the largest minority groups in the United States?
   ___ ___

Turn to the next page to check your responses.

1. *Objective:* Given Sunday comics, be able to list all of the individual strip titles within the classifications of dry humor, light humor, romance, mysteries, detective, adventure, sociological, or religious.

   Criterion Item: Check the comic strip that deals with light humor.
   (a) Dick Tracy   (c) Mary Worth
   (b) Nancy   (d) Little Orphan Annie   ___ ✓

2. *Objective:* Be able to list five major pieces of legislation that were passed in the United States during the Progressive Era (1900–1917).

   Criterion Item: Underline five of the following pieces of twentieth-century legislation that were passed during the Progressive Era (1900–1917).
   (a) Pure Food and   (d) Hepburn Act
       Drug Act   (e) Prohibition Act
   (b) Federal Reserve Act (f) Social Security Act
   (c) Underwood Tariff   ___ ✓

3. *Objective:* Given ten minority groups in the United States, list at least eight of them in order according to total population.

   Criterion Item: What are eight of the largest minority groups in the United States?   ___ ✓

1. No match. The objective asks the student to *list* (main intent is recall); the test item asks the student to *check* (main intent is recognition). The performances do not match, and there is no need to look further. If the performances had matched, there would still be no match, as the conditions are considerably different. The objective says the student will be given some comics; the item only lists the names of comic strips. Not the same.

2. No match. The objective says *list* (recall) and the item says *underline* (recognize).

3. No match. The performances don't match. The objective says the learner will be given something and he or she is to *rearrange* them. The item asks the learner to *recall*. Moreover, the objective asks for an arrangement *in order* according to population; the item only asks for a list of the largest. The item therefore tests for less than the entire objective.

Practice Items

4. *Objective:* Given the original price and the sale price of an article, be able to compute the rate of discount of the article to the nearest whole percent.

   Criterion Item: A boat normally selling for $1,500 is on sale for $1,200. What is the rate of discount to the nearest whole percent?   ____ ____

5. *Objective:* Be able to perform a neurological examination using proper techniques and equipment.

   Criterion Item: Describe the equipment and procedures used to conduct a neurological examination.   ____ ____

6. *Objective:* For each of these procedures (craniotomy, laminectomy), describe the locations and functions of the scrub nurse and assistants.

   Criterion Item: Describe the location and function of the scrub nurse and assistants for each of these surgical procedures:
   (a) Craniotomy   (b) Laminectomy   ____ ____

7. *Objective:* Having written a broad intent (goal) you feel worthy of achievement, be able to write the objective(s) which, if achieved, will cause you to agree that the goal is also achieved. (That is, write the operational definition of a goal you consider worthy of achievement.)

   Criterion Item: Which of the following goals do you feel is most worthy of achievement in today's society?
   (a) Good citizenship   (c) Law and order
   (b) Population reduction (d) Honest government   ____ ____

8. *Objective:* Be able to list four possible elements of kidnapping that are outlined in the Penal Code, Section 208.

   Criterion Item: Joe has taken Tom across the state line against his will. Which section of the Penal Code outlines this action as a kidnapping?   ____ ____

Turn to the next page to check your responses.

4. *Objective:* Given the original price and the sale price of an article, be able to compute the rate of discount of the article to the nearest whole percent.

   Criterion Item: A boat normally selling for $1,500 is on sale for $1,200. What is the rate of discount to the nearest whole percent?   ✓ ___

5. *Objective:* Be able to perform a neurological examination using proper techniques and equipment.

   Criterion Item: Describe the equipment and procedures used to conduct a neurological examination.   ___ ✓

6. *Objective:* For each of these procedures (craniotomy, laminectomy), describe the locations and functions of the scrub nurse and assistants.

   Criterion Item: Describe the location and function of the scrub nurse and assistants for each of these surgical procedures:
   (a) Craniotomy   (b) Laminectomy   ✓ ___

7. *Objective:* Having written a broad intent (goal) you feel worthy of achievement, be able to write the objective(s) which, if achieved, will cause you to agree that the goal is also achieved. (That is, write the operational definition of a goal you consider worthy of achievement.)

   Criterion Item: Which of the following goals do you feel is most worthy of achievement in today's society?
   (a) Good citizenship   (c) Law and order
   (b) Population reduction (d) Honest government   ___ ✓

8. *Objective:* Be able to list four possible elements of kidnapping that are outlined in the Penal Code, Section 208.

   Criterion Item: Joe has taken Tom across the state line against his will. Which section of the Penal Code outlines this action as a kidnapping?   ___ ✓

4. A match. Both objective and item ask the student to find the rate of discount, and the item asks for that performance under the same conditions described by the objective. Additional items might be used, of course, but each would need to be of this type.

5. Not on your life. Describing equipment and procedures is not at all the same as performing an examination. No match.

6. A match. The item matches the objective in every way. Notice that you didn't have to be big in medical knowledge to tell whether the item matches the objective. This isn't always true, but it should be comforting to know that you can spot good or bad items in fields other than your own.

7. No match. The objective calls for writing, and that appears to be the main intent. The item clearly does not ask for the same thing. To be suitable, the item would have to ask the student to write objectives that define a goal. No other item form would suffice.

8. No match. The objective says to list (recall) four elements. The item offers a situation and asks the student to recall a section that applies.

Practice Items

WHICH, IF ANY

Following are three objectives and a set of test items for each. If an item matches the objective, check the YES column to the right. If not, check the NO column.

Is the item appropriate?

YES   NO

Objective: Be able to construct a parallelogram of any given dimensions that is accurate to within 1.5 cm.

Test Items:

1. Define *parallelogram*.   ____   ____

2. Describe the difference between a parallelogram and a rectangle.   ____   ____

3. Look at the following figures and draw a circle around the one that is a parallelogram.   ____   ____

4. Draw a parallelogram whose sides are 11 cm and 13 cm in length.   ____   ____

5. Construct a parallelogram whose sides are 5 cm and 7 cm in length, accurate to ± 1.5 cm.   ____   ____

Turn the page to check your responses.

Objective: Be able to construct a parallelogram of any given dimensions that is accurate to within 1.5 cm.

Test Items:

1. Define *parallelogram*.   ___   ✓

2. Describe the difference between a parallelogram and a rectangle.   ___   ✓

3. Look at the following figures and draw a circle around the one that is a parallelogram.   ___   ✓

4. Draw a parallelogram whose sides are 11 cm and 13 cm in length.   ___   ✓

5. Construct a parallelogram whose sides are 5 cm and 7 cm in length, accurate to ±1.5 cm.   ✓   ___

1. One of the least appropriate items imaginable (though popular). "But students don't really understand parallelograms unless they can define one," one might cry in anguish. All right. But if you feel that way about it there are two things to do. Either teach your students the definition as enrichment or background and don't test on it, or write an objective that reflects your intent.

2. No match. This might make a fine diagnostic item—that is, it might be useful in finding out why a student has *not* achieved the objective—but it is not appropriate for finding out if he or she *has* achieved the objective.

3. Not appropriate. Again, this item might be good for discovering that students had not achieved the objective because they couldn't recognize a parallelogram when they saw one, but it won't tell whether they can construct one.

4. Well, if you are non-mathematical like me, this item would be okay. A mathematician, however, makes a distinction between drawing and constructing. Drawing is what one does when sketching freehand; constructing is what one does when drawing accurately with the use of instruments. A mathematician would say they are not the same.

5. Appropriate. Finally. Use as many such items as you feel are necessary to sample the stimulus range, but all items have to ask students to construct a parallelogram. As stated, the objective says to construct "a" parallelogram. If you intended that students' performance would be considered acceptable only if they correctly construct, say, four out of five parallelograms to given dimensions, that criterion might well be written into the objective.

Practice Items

Objective: Be able to read a domestic electric power meter correctly to the nearest unit and record your readings on the appropriate page of the meter reader's log.

Test Items:

1. Record on the appropriate page of your log the readings of each of these ten domestic meters to the nearest unit.   ____   ____

2. Of the five dials on the domestic meter, which records "thousand of units"?   ____   ____

3. Look at this picture of a dial. What is the reading?   ____   ____

4. Look at the dials on these domestic meters. What are the readings?   ____   ____

5. Define *kilowatt-hour*.   ____   ____

Turn the page to check your responses.

123

Objective: Be able to read a domestic electric power meter correctly to the nearest unit and record your readings on the appropriate page of the meter reader's log.

Test Items:

1. Record on the appropriate page of your log the readings of each of these ten domestic meters to the nearest unit.   ✓   ___

2. Of the five dials on the domestic meter, which records "thousand of units"?   ___   ✓

3. Look at this picture of a dial. What is the reading?   ___   ✓

4. Look at the dials on these domestic meters. What are the readings?   ___   ✓

5. Define *kilowatt-hour*.   ___   ✓

1. An appropriate item. The objective says "read and record" to the nearest unit, and the test item says "record" to the nearest unit. Presumably meter readers can't record what they haven't read, so I would consider this item a match. If you think I am assuming too much, then a small modification of the test item would be in order. And if you feel that way, hooray!

2. This might be a good diagnostic item and useful for determining whether a person who had not achieved the objective was having trouble because he or she didn't know which dial was showing what, but it is not adequate for finding out whether one can read and record complete readings in a log book.

3. This one tests for *part* of the objective, to be sure, but not for the entire objective. You may learn that a person can read properly, but you won't find out if he or she can read and then record to the nearest unit.

4. Same problem as Item 3. If an item is not appropriate for testing achievement of an objective, adding several more items of the same type will not improve matters.

5. Not appropriate. What is the main intent of the objective? Read and record. What does the test item ask for? A definition. They are not the same. The only appropriate item is one that will ask the student to read and record.

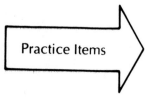
Practice Items

This one is a little more subtle than it may appear. Follow the checklist and you shouldn't have any trouble.

	Is the item appropriate?	
	YES	NO

Objective: Be able to type a business letter in accordance with the standards described in Company Manual 12-21.

Test Items:

1. Describe the five basic elements of a business letter. ___ ___

2. Sort the ten sample letters into piles representing those that are written in accordance with Company standards, and those that are not. ___ ___

3. On the five sample letters given, circle any errors or items not in accordance with standards of good grammar. ___ ___

4. Describe in a paragraph the rationale for the business letter standards currently in effect. ___ ___

5. From the rough copy given, type a business letter in the form set out by Manual 12-21. ___ ___

Turn the page to check your responses.

Objective: Be able to type a business letter in accordance with the standards described in Company Manual 12-21.

Test Items:

1. Describe the five basic elements of a business letter.   ___   ✓

2. Sort the ten sample letters into piles representing those that are written in accordance with Company standards, and those that are not.   ___   ✓

3. On the five sample letters given, circle any errors or items not in accordance with standards of good grammar.   ___   ✓

4. Describe in a paragraph the rationale for the business letter standards currently in effect.   ___   ✓

5. From the rough copy given, type a business letter in the form set out by Manual 12-21.   ___   ✓

1. The objective says *type* and the test item says *describe*. Not the same, so you needn't even bother to look at the conditions.

2. Not appropriate. Typing is not the same as sorting. During instruction it might be useful to sharpen students' ability to recognize letters written according to company standards by having them sort sample letters into piles of those that are okay and those that are not. Or, it might be a good diagnostic item for finding out why a student *cannot* type letters as desired. But it is not appropriate for testing achievement of the objective.

3. Not appropriate. Same comment as for Item 2.

4. Neither the performances nor the conditions match. (To chant "I like to vary the type of test items I use to make my tests more interesting," doesn't make this item any more acceptable.)

5. Here's the sticky one. First off, the performances match. Right? Both the objective and the test item ask students to type a letter. So far so good. But what about the conditions? The way I read it, the test item asks for the performance of letter typing under conditions different from those called for by the objective; the test item imposes an additional requirement when it requires students to do their letter typing from *rough copy*. If you don't type much, this point could easily slip by; but regular letter typists know that it can be very difficult to have to type from scraggly handwritten copy. Either the objective or the item needs to be changed to match the other.

Practice Items

FIX IT

Below are pairs of statements, each consisting of an alleged objective and an allegedly suitable test item. Edit (fix, repair) either the objective or the item, or both, so that the item is appropriate for testing achievement of the objective.

1. *Objective:* Be able to describe to a customer the services provided by the bank.

   Criterion Item: Which of the following services are available to bank customers?
   (a) Checking accounts
   (b) Savings accounts
   (c) Neck massages
   (d) Manicures
   (e) Loans
   (f) Mortgages

2. *Objective:* Be able to measure, with the use of a metric balance, to the nearest gram.

   Criterion Item: Record on paper the weight of the following objects: dime, quarter, a new pencil, a new rubber eraser, and a piece of chalk.

Turn the page to check your revisions.

1. Here you need to match performances, because the objective is asking for what appears to be verbal recall (describe to a customer) and the item merely asks for recognition. Then again, it isn't clear from the objective whether students will be expected to describe each of the services provided from a list available to them or whether they will have to recall the services without the use of references. I would make the objective and item read the following way, though your own version is acceptable if the performances and conditions match.

   Objective: Using the list of services provided, be able to describe verbally each of the bank services that is available to the customer. For each service, present the following information: (a) what the service is and what it provides, (b) how the service may be obtained, and (c) the cost of the service to the customer.

   Criterion Item: Using the tape recorder provided and a list of bank services, record your description of each service. Include in each description (a) the extent of the service, (b) information on how it may be obtained, and (c) cost.

2. This is more a case of sloppy wording rather than of items that don't match. The objective is reasonably clear. The item isn't bad either, except that strictly speaking it doesn't say students have to use the balance. Tidying up gives you something like this:

   Objective: Using a metric balance, be able to measure the weight of any given object, accurate to the nearest gram.

   Criterion Item: Weigh these objects with the metric balance and record, to the nearest gram, the weights on your answer sheet: dime, quarter, a new pencil, a new rubber eraser, piece of chalk.

Try One More

3. *Objective:* Be able to demonstrate an understanding of the difference between Scotch and saki by making some of each.

Criterion Item: On Table 3 are ten numbered glasses. Sip the content of each, and beside the appropriate number on your answer sheet write whether the sample was Scotch or saki.

Turn the page to check your revisions.

3. This objective is stated in a treacherous manner because of the words "demonstrate an understanding of the difference." The word *demonstrate* always makes a statement sound terribly precise and behaviorally oriented even when it isn't. The trap is that it doesn't say anything about *kind* of difference. In this case what kind of difference does the objective want people to be able to demonstrate an understanding of? Difference in shape or size of the bottles, difference in labels, difference in manufacturing process? It simply doesn't say. The objective implies that it is interested in the manufacturing process ("by making some of each"), but the item is interested in taste difference. One suspects that the item is the more reasonable intent and the "making some of each" in the objective is merely a bad selection of an indicator. If that is the way you see it, then you might modify these statements as follows:

Objective: Given unmarked samples of Scotch and saki, be able to say which is which by taste.

Criterion Item: On Table 3 are five numbered glasses. Sip the content of each, and beside the appropriate number on your answer sheet write whether the sample was Scotch or saki.

(What would be a reasonable criterion of success? Steady there. One lugubrious colleague would prefer 99 out of 100 sips correct, but another one, a totalteeler, would rather avoid the issue altogether. If it's *your* objective, *you* say what you would accept to make you willing to certify your students as satisfactory saki sippers.)

8 | Got a Match?

It's time to find out whether the objective of the book has been achieved, to discover whether you are able to recognize criterion items that would be suitable for determining whether an objective has been reached. How shall this be done? Shall I ask you to trace the history of testing, or to write an essay on the significance of the multiple-choice item? Mmmm. I've got it! I'll write an item that asks you to compare and contrast norm-referenced with criterion-referenced testing. If you can do that, I can conclude that you *really* understand the subject. Right?

Oh. You're going to be fussy about it, I see, so I'd better try to practice what I've been trying to get you to practice. On the other hand the temptation is great to slip in a few items that test the limit or breadth of your understanding. You know how it is—if I just use items that test for the objective, you might get them all correct. And then where would I be? I'd have to write some "harder" items so you didn't get the idea the "course" was too easy. Right?

Oh. Wrong again? All right, enough is enough, but I just couldn't resist one last chance to make the point that it isn't exactly being honest with students to tell them you want them to be able to do one thing and then test them for something else.

The thing to do is offer you some criterion items, each of which matches the objective of this book. To make it easier for you to decide whether I succeed in doing so, I will repeat the book's objective here.

Be able to discriminate (select, point to) *the test items that are appropriate for testing the achievement of an instructional objective, when given*

(a) *An objective*
(b) *One or more allegedly suitable test items*
(c) *The Objective/Item Checklist*

SECTION I. YES, NO, OR CAN'T TELL

The following pairs of statements each consist of an objective and a test item. If the test item *is* appropriate for testing achievement of the objective, check the YES column to the right. If the item is *not* appropriate, check the NO column. If you can't apply the matching procedure because the objective is too fuzzy (i.e., doesn't state a performance), check the CAN'T TELL column.

Is the item suitable?

	YES	NO	CAN'T TELL

1. *Objective:* Given a performance of an instrumental or vocal melody containing a melodic or rhythmic error, and given the score for the melody, be able to point out the error.

   Criterion Item: The instructor will play the melody of the attached musical score on the piano and will make an error either in rhythm or melody. Raise your hand when the error occurs.   ___ ___   ___

(Continued on next page.)

2. *Objective:* Given mathematical equations containing one unknown, be able to solve for the unknown.

   Criterion Item: Sam weighs 97 kilos. He weighs 3.5 kilos more than Barney. How much does Barney weigh? ___ ___ ___

3. *Objective:* Be able to demonstrate familiarity with sexual anatomy and physiology.

   Criterion Item: Draw and label a sketch of the male and female reproductive systems. ___ ___ ___

4. *Objective:* Given any one of the computers in our product line, in its original carton, be able to install and adjust the machine, preparing it for use. Criteria: The machine shows normal indication, and the area is free of debris and cartons.

   Criterion Item: Select one of the cartons containing one of our Model XX computers, and install it for the secretary in Room 45. Make sure it is ready for use and the area is left clean. ___ ___ ___

5. *Objective:* When given a set of paragraphs (that use words within your vocabulary), some of which are missing topic sentences, be able to identify the paragraphs without topic sentences.

   Criterion Item: Turn to page 29 in your copy of *Silas Marner*. Underline the topic sentence of each paragraph on that page. ___ ___ ___

(Continued on next page.)

6. *Note:* Not every objective comes in a single sentence. Many objectives that describe a complex or higher-order skill need several sentences, as the following one illustrates. Use your checklist and the objective should fall easily into place.

Objective: Given a chapter in a textbook, be able to derive and draw a shorthand pyramid of objectives. Each shorthand objective must state the action required of the student, and any important conditions under which the action is to be performed. Criteria will not be specified. The pyramid should extend through at least two levels of subordinate objectives or to the assumed entry level skills of the target population, whichever chain is longer.

Criterion Item: Select a chapter in a textbook of your choice, and derive the objectives, if any, that the chapter appears to be accomplishing. The text should be one used in your own discipline or subject specialty. Prepare a shorthand pyramid of those objectives. Show the main action and any important conditions, but do not include criteria of acceptable performance. Extend the pyramid through at least two levels of subordinate objectives or to the assumed entry level skills of the target population, whichever chain is longer. —— ——   ——

7. *Objective:* Given live or filmed demonstrations of various actions, be able to tell which actions are in violation of Section 415, Disturbing the Peace.

(Continued on next page.)

7. *(Continued.)*

   Criterion Item: Check each of the following actions that represents a violation of Section 415, Disturbing the Peace.

   (a) Helen fires a pistol into the ground in her own backyard.

   (b) Hal and Joe are having a fist fight in the corner bar.

   (c) Sarah, wanting to sleep, asks her neighbor to turn down a noisy TV. The neighbor turns it up to full volume.
   ___ ___   ___

8. *Objective:* Be able to taxi any C series aircraft, according to criteria stated in the Flight Crew Checklist, without performing steps that are unnecessary or a danger to the aircraft, its crew, or other aircraft in the area.

   Criterion Item: Following is a list of steps to be completed before taxi of the C-124A aircraft. Check (√) those that are correct, and X those that are unnecessary or incorrect.

   ___(a) Hydraulic pressure "WITHIN LIMITS"

   ___(b) Brakes "CHECKED"

   ___(c) Flight instruments "COPILOT'S CHECKED" (CP), "PILOT'S CHECKED" (S)

   ___(d) Scanner's report "ENGINE CHECKED" (S)

   ___(e) CHECK COMPLETED (CP)
   ___ ___   ___

(Continued on next page.)

9. *Objective:* The competent nurse is able to observe any patient and tell which of the patient's characteristics should be responded to and which should be ignored (i.e., not responded to).

   Criterion Item: Describe to your instructor five of the patient's characteristics that should be responded to and at least five characteristics to which you should withhold a response. ____ ____ ____

10. *Objective:* Given a Model 31 Brainwasher, a standard tool kit, a standard spares kit, test equipment, and at least one symptom of a common malfunction, be able to return the system to normal operation. Criteria: The system functions within specifications. There is no cosmetic or structural damage to the system or to the immediate area. No more than one unnecessary spare is used. All paperwork is completed correctly, and no complaints are filed by client personnel.

   Criterion Item: The Model 31 Brainwasher in the test room can be turned on, but the washing fluid leaks onto the brain-removal mechanism during the wash cycle. Return the machine to normal operating condition. The tool kit, spares, and test equipment beside the machine are available as you need them. Call the instructor when you have finished. ____ ____ ____

SECTION II. WHICH, IF ANY

Following are four objectives, and a set of test items for each. If an item is appropriate for testing the objective, check the YES column at the right. If not, check the NO column. If an item is in some way obscure so that you can't apply the matching procedure, check the CAN'T TELL column.

Is the item suitable?

	YES	NO	CAN'T TELL

A. *Objective:* When approached by a prospective customer, be able to respond in a positive manner (with a smile, a suitable greeting, and a pleasant tone of voice).

Criterion Items:

1. Describe the three basic characteristics of a positive response to the approach of a prospective customer. ___ ___ ___

2. Watch the following ten film clips and write down the numbers of those that represent a correct response to the approach of a prospective customer. ___ ___ ___

3. When the instructor hangs the "customer" sign around his neck and approaches you, make the positive response to the approach of a prospective customer. ___ ___ ___

4. When approached by each of five students selected by the instructor, make the appropriate (positive) response to customer approach. ___ ___ ___

B. *Objective:* Given the stock market quotations from any current newspaper for two different dates and a schedule of brokerage fees, be able to compute the profit or loss resulting from the "buy" of a given number of shares on the earliest of the two dates and a "sell" on the latest.

Criterion Items:

1. In Packet A are stock market quotations from newspapers of different days and a schedule of brokerage fees. For each of the five stocks circled, calculate the profit or loss that would result from buying the stock on the earlier date and selling it on the later date. Write the profit or loss in the spaces provided. ___ ___ ___

2. In Packet A are stock market quotations from newspapers of different days and a schedule of brokerage fees. Describe in writing how brokerage fees are applied to any stock sale. ___ ___ ___

3. Using the schedule of brokerage fees provided, write an example to illustrate how profit and loss is computed for sale of stocks. ___ ___ ___

4. Explain the meaning of each of the entries shown for the stocks circled on the newspaper stock pages attached. ___ ___ ___

5. Describe the procedure for buying and selling a stock. ___ ___ ___

C. *Objective:* Given a malfunctioning amplifier of any design, one symptom, reference materials, and tools, be able to repair the unit so that it functions within design specifications.

Criterion Items:

1. Design an amplifier that meets the specifications shown on the attached sheet. Show the values and tolerances for each component. ___ ___ ___

2. List the three most common troubles to be expected from each of the amplifier designs contained in Packet A. ___ ___ ___

3. Attached to this sheet are the schematic diagrams for three different kinds of amplifiers. A red circle is drawn around one component of each amplifier. On the bottom of the page write the symptom(s) that would show up if the circled components were malfunctioning. ___ ___ ___

4. At Stations A, B, and C are three amplifiers. The tag on each amplifier describes one symptom of the trouble that has been inserted. Using the tools and references provided at each station, repair each amplifier. ___ ___ ___

5. At Stations A, B, and C are three amplifiers. The tag on each amplifier describes one symptom of the trouble that has been inserted. On the page provided, describe the steps you would take to clear the trouble and put the amplifier back into operation. ___ ___ ___

143

D. *Objective:* Given a set of diagrams or slides of correctly angled periodontal probe calibrations, write the correct probe reading of each, rounded to the next highest millimeter.*

Criterion Items:

1. On a periodontal probe, which marks are missing? ___ ___ ___

2. Look at the slides in Envelope D, and write down the probe reading shown in each. Round your answer to the next highest millimeter. ___ ___ ___

3. In Envelope E are slides showing probes that have been inserted into the sulcus. For each slide, tell whether any precautions have been overlooked and, if so, which ones. ___ ___ ___

---

* Objective and criterion items courtesy of Pipe & Associates.

RESPONSES

Here is how I would respond to the items on the previous pages. Perhaps you would like to compare your responses with mine.

Turn to the next page.

1. *Objective:* Given a performance of an instrumental or vocal melody containing a melodic or rhythmic error, and given the score for the melody, be able to point out the error.

   Criterion Item: The instructor will play the melody of the attached musical score on the piano and will make an error either in rhythm or melody. Raise your hand when the error occurs.   ✓

2. *Objective:* Given mathematical equations containing one unknown, be able to solve for the unknown.

   Criterion Item: Sam weighs 97 kilos. He weighs 3.5 kilos more than Barney. How much does Barney weigh?   ✓

3. *Objective:* Be able to demonstrate familiarity with sexual anatomy and physiology.

   Criterion Item: Draw and label a sketch of the male and female reproductive systems.   ✓

4. *Objective:* Given any one of the computers in our product line, in its original carton, be able to install and adjust the machine, preparing it for use. Criteria: The machine shows normal indication, and the area is free of debris and cartons.

   Criterion Item: Select one of the cartons containing one of our Model XX computers, and install it for the secretary in Room 45. Make sure it is ready for use and the area is left clean.   ✓

Section I. Yes, No, or Can't Tell

1. The item is suitable. The objective wants students to be able to recognize errors in the performance of a piece of music for which they are given the score; it wants them to detect *(discriminate, locate, spot)* errors between the rendition and the score. The item asks for the same. True, the indicator stated in the objective is "point out," and the test item asks for hand raising. Since hand raising is a simple and direct method for indicating the main intent, the item is suitable.

2. Not suitable. This one represents a common mismatch between teaching and testing. Students are expected to be able to solve a given type of mathematical equation. Not only does the item not provide an equation to solve, it asks for a different skill. Solving an equation is not the same as setting up an equation from a word problem. Neither the performance nor the conditions match.

3. Can't tell. What is someone doing when demonstrating his or her familiarity with sexual anatomy? Don't answer that. But unless the objective answers it there is no way to tell if the item is appropriate for checking out success at achievement of the objective.

4. Suitable. The objective asks someone to install and adjust, as does the test item. The objective does not include conditions regarding the environment in which the machine is to be installed, but since the environment (the secretary in Room 45) doesn't require more student skill than implied by the objective, the conditions match.

5. *Objective:* When given a set of paragraphs (that use words within your vocabulary), some of which are missing
topic sentences, be able to identify the
paragraphs without topic sentences.

    Criterion Item: Turn to page 29 in your
copy of *Silas Marner.* Underline the topic
sentence of each paragraph on that page. ___ ✓ ___

6. *Objective:* Given a chapter in a textbook, be able to derive and draw a shorthand pyramid of objectives. Each
shorthand objective must state the action
required of the student, and any important conditions under which the action is
to be performed. Criteria will not be specified. The pyramid should extend through
at least two levels of subordinate objectives or to the assumed entry level skills of
the target population, whichever chain is
longer.

    Criterion Item: Select a chapter in a
textbook of your choice, and derive the
objectives, if any, that the chapter appears
to be accomplishing. The text should be
one used in your own discipline or subject
specialty. Prepare a shorthand pyramid of
those objectives. Show the main action
and any important conditions, but do not
include criteria of acceptable performance. Extend the pyramid through at
least two levels of subordinate objectives or
to the assumed entry level skills of the target population, whichever chain is longer. ✓ ___ ___

148

5. Not appropriate. The objective asks students to identify paragraphs without topic sentences; the item asks them to identify (by underlining) topic sentences. Not the same.

6. Suitable. The objective asks that learners be able to construct a shorthand pyramid of objectives (i.e., an objectives hierarchy) from a chapter in a textbook; the item asks for the same. And though the wording is slightly different between objective and item, conditions match as well.

   Why does the item look so much like the objective? You know the answer to that. When the performance stated in the objective is mainly overt and at the same time the main intent, there is only one type of item suitable for assessing achievement of the objective—the type that asks learners to do just what the objective says. As you know, it is only when the objective performance is visible and a main intent that test items look similar; whenever the objective main intent is covert, an indicator must be used, regardless of whether that covert main intent is mainly cognitive or affective. In these instances the test items look noticeably different from the objective.

7. *Objective:* Given live or filmed demonstrations of various actions, be able to tell which actions are in violation of Section 415, Disturbing the Peace.

Criterion Item: Check each of the following actions that represents a violation of Section 415, Disturbing the Peace.

(a) Helen fires a pistol into the ground in her own backyard.

(b) Hal and Joe are having a fist fight in the corner bar.

(c) Sarah, wanting to sleep, asks her neighbor to turn down a noisy TV. The neighbor turns it up to full volume.   ___ ✓ ___

8. *Objective:* Be able to taxi any C series aircraft, according to criteria stated in the Flight Crew Checklist, without performing steps that are unnecessary or a danger to the aircraft, its crew, or other aircraft in the area.

Criterion Item: Following is a list of steps to be completed before taxi of the C-124A aircraft. Check (√) those that are correct, and X those that are unnecessary or incorrect.

___(a) Hydraulic pressure "WITHIN LIMITS"

___(b) Brakes "CHECKED"

___(c) Flight instruments "COPILOT'S CHECKED" (CP), "PILOT'S CHECKED" (S)

___(d) Scanner's report "ENGINE CHECKED" (S)

___(e) CHECK COMPLETED (CP)   ___ ✓ ___

7. Not suitable. Both objective and item want students to be able to identify actions that are violations of Section 415. The objective, however, wants them to be able to do their identifying in response to live or filmed demonstrations; the item asks for the identifying in response to verbal descriptions of situations. Not the same. If a learner responded well to the item as written, would you be able to conclude that he or she could handle real situations as well? I'm not sure. What is clear is that the item demands an *inference* about whether the objective has actually been accomplished.

8. Not appropriate. Taxiing an aircraft and recognizing written steps to be completed before taxiing are not the same.

   Again, the item might be useful as a diagnostic item to reveal one of the reasons the taxiing was not accomplished as desired. Or it might be useful as a pre-flight checkout to find out if a student is ready to try taxiing. After all, you wouldn't let any student taxi an expensive aircraft (they all are) unless you felt confident that he or she knew what to do. But that doesn't slice any bananas. If you want to find out if students can taxi, ask them to taxi.

9. *Objective:* The competent nurse is able to observe any patient and tell which of the patient's characteristics should be responded to and which should be ignored (i.e., not responded to).

   Criterion Item: Describe to your instructor five of the patient's characteristics that should be responded to and at least five characteristics to which you should withhold a response. ___ ✓ ___

10. *Objective:* Given a Model 31 Brainwasher, a standard tool kit, a standard spares kit, test equipment, and at least one symptom of a common malfunction, be able to return the system to normal operation. Criteria: The system functions within specifications. There is no cosmetic or structural damage to the system or to the immediate area. No more than one unnecessary spare is used. All paperwork is completed correctly, and no complaints are filed by client personnel.

    Criterion Item: The Model 31 Brainwasher in the test room can be turned on, but the washing fluid leaks onto the brain-removal mechanism during the wash cycle. Return the machine to normal operating condition. The tool kit, spares, and test equipment beside the machine are available as you need them. Call the instructor when you have finished. ___ ✓ ___

9. Same as Number 8. Not appropriate. The item asks students to recall some characteristics, while the objective asks them to tell *(identify)* characteristics of real patients. Not the same.

10. Close, but no bell ringer. The performances match; both objective and item ask students to repair a machine when shown at least one symptom of malfunction. And *some* of the conditions match. But the objective asks that paperwork be completed; the test item asks that the instructor be called when the task is completed. The objective asks that no complaints be filed by client personnel; the test is clearly conducted in a classroom rather than on client premises.

Now, it may be *necessary* or practical (convenient) to do the testing in a classroom instead of on client premises. If that is the case, so be it. But that wouldn't change the fact that the conditions don't match. If this test item were used as the means of finding out whether the objective was achieved, the evaluators could only *infer*—make an educated guess—whether the objective was achieved. It might be a pretty good inference about whether a student could repair the machine, but it would be a poor inference about whether a student could work correctly on client premises or complete the necessary paperwork.

A. *Objective:* When approached by a prospective customer, be able to respond in a positive manner (with a smile, a suitable greeting, and a pleasant tone of voice).

Criterion Items:

1. Describe the three basic characteristics of a positive response to the approach of a prospective customer. ___ ✓ ___

2. Watch the following ten film clips and write down the numbers of those that represent a correct response to the approach of a prospective customer. ___ ✓ ___

3. When the instructor hangs the "customer" sign around his neck and approaches you, make the positive response to the approach of a prospective customer. ✓ ___ ___

4. When approached by each of five students selected by the instructor, make the appropriate (positive) response to customer approach. ✓ ___ ___

Section II. Which, If Any

A. 1. Not appropriate. Responding in a positive manner is not the same as describing characteristics. Neither performances nor conditions match.

2. No good. Recognizing proper approaches in a film is not the same as responding to a prospective customer. Items 1 and 2 may provide some good practice in developing parts of the desired skill, but they are not useful for finding out if the skill *has* been developed.

3. Pretty good. The item asks for a response to an instructor who is pretending to be a prospective customer, and so the item is asking for a simulation of the desired performance. Or is it? Maybe the instructor *is* a prospective customer. You would need to know more about the actual situation to be sure. I would accept this item as suitable, but if you feel the urge to revise it, I will be happy to cheer you on.

4. This one is very similar to the one above, except that it asks for the response to be made five times instead of one, and asks that the response be made to students instead of the instructor. The performances match, and the conditions seem very close. If you would not be willing to accept the item, how could you change it?

B. *Objective:* Given the stock market quotations from any current newspaper for two different dates and a schedule of brokerage fees, be able to compute the profit or loss resulting from the "buy" of a given number of shares on the earliest of the two dates and a "sell" on the latest.

Criterion Items:

1. In Packet A are stock market quotations from newspapers of different days and a schedule of brokerage fees. For each of the five stocks circled, calculate the profit or loss that would result from buying the stock on the earlier date and selling it on the later date. Write the profit or loss in the spaces provided.   ✓ ___ ___

2. In Packet A are stock market quotations from newspapers of different days and a schedule of brokerage fees. Describe in writing how brokerage fees are applied to any stock sale.   ___ ✓ ___

3. Using the schedule of brokerage fees provided, write an example to illustrate how profit and loss is computed for sale of stocks.   ___ ✓ ___

4. Explain the meaning of each of the entries shown for the stocks circled on the newspaper stock pages attached.   ___ ✓ ___

5. Describe the procedure for buying and selling a stock.   ___ ✓ ___

156

B. 1. Item is suitable. The main intent of the objective is that students be able to compute profit and loss on a stock sale. Though the objective doesn't state an indicator, I think you can safely assume that writing down the result of the calculation is the simplest and most direct indicator that would tell you if the computation is correct. If you don't think you can so assume, I would be happy to support your urge (is that a performance?) to modify the item a little.

2. No good. Describing a procedure is not the same as carrying out the procedure.

3. No good. Writing an example is not the same as calculating profit or loss.

4. Not adequate. But students couldn't calculate profit or loss unless they knew the meaning of the newspaper stock entries, could they? Of course not. But that's not the point, is it? If your true intent is for students to be able to describe entries, then that is what the objective should say.

5. Not adequate. Describing a procedure is not the same as carrying out a procedure.

C. *Objective:* Given a malfunctioning amplifier of any design, one symptom, reference materials, and tools, be able to repair the unit so that it functions within design specifications.

Criterion Items:

1. Design an amplifier that meets the specifications shown on the attached sheet. Show the values and tolerances for each component. ___ ✓ ___

2. List the three most common troubles to be expected from each of the amplifier designs contained in Packet A. ___ ✓ ___

3. Attached to this sheet are the schematic diagrams for three different kinds of amplifiers. A red circle is drawn around one component of each amplifier. On the bottom of the page write the symptom(s) that would show up if the circled components were malfunctioning. ___ ✓ ___

4. At Stations A, B, and C are three amplifiers. The tag on each amplifier describes one symptom of the trouble that has been inserted. Using the tools and references provided at each station, repair each amplifier. ✓ ___ ___

5. At Stations A, B, and C are three amplifiers. The tag on each amplifier describes one symptom of the trouble that has been inserted. On the page provided, describe the steps you would take to clear the trouble and put the amplifier back into operation. ___ ✓ ___

C. 1. Not adequate. The objective wants students to be able to repair, and the item asks for design. Not the same thing at all. What would you say to someone who said, "But students don't really understand how to fix one unless they can design one"? (Now don't be too nasty.) Hopefully, you would remind that person that while his or her comment has a grain of truth, it is not relevant to the point. If you want to know if learners can fix, ask them to fix.

2. Not adequate. Listing (recalling) common troubles is not the same as repairing an ailing amplifier.

3. Sounds good, but it won't do. Actually the item is backwards from the objective, in the sense that the objective asks students to go from symptom to trouble and the item asks them to go from trouble to symptom.

4. Item is adequate (at last). But where does the item writer get off asking for *three* repair jobs? Why not only one? Or ten? I dunno. A sharp writer may have asked for three because with three he or she could sample the range of amplifiers and troubles learners will be expected to handle in the immediate future.

5. Not adequate. Talking a good job isn't the same as doing a good job.

D. *Objective:* Given a set of diagrams or slides of correctly angled periodontal probe calibrations, write the correct probe reading of each, rounded to the next highest millimeter.*

Criterion Items:

1. On a periodontal probe, which marks are missing? ___ ✓ ___

2. Look at the slides in Envelope D, and write down the probe reading shown in each. Round your answer to the next highest millimeter. ✓ ___ ___

3. In Envelope E are slides showing probes that have been inserted into the sulcus. For each slide, tell whether any precautions have been over-looked and, if so, which ones. ___ ✓ ___

---

* Objective and criterion items courtesy of Pipe & Associates.

D. 1. Not adequate. Even though you may not know what a periodontal probe is, you can see that telling which marks are missing is not the same as writing correct probe readings. (If a dentist could peer through a periodontal probe, would that make it a perioscope? No . . . Don't throw it!)

2. Suitable. Both item and objective ask learners to write correct probe readings. What's that you say? You don't know that the slides in the envelope show correctly handled insertions? Ahh, you *are* getting to be the sly one. You are correct, of course; we have to assume that the slides represent the objective conditions to call it a match.

3. No again. Describing precautions is not the same as writing correct probe readings.

HOW'D YOU DO?

How is your skill at recognizing items relevant to objectives? Are you as good at it as some, better than most? By now you know my answer to this question is that it doesn't matter. What matters is whether you can or cannot perform the skill with adequacy. What's adequate? Well, if I were to have to decide whether you had met my criterion of success, I would do so on this basis:

At least 8 of 10 items correct from Section I, correct items to include items 1, 3, 5, 7, 8, and 10.

and

At least 15 of 17 items correct from Section II, correct items to include items A3 or A4, B1, C4, and D2.

A final word about the matching of test items to objectives:

Trial
Summary

Trial was held on January 17, 1984, in Superior Court of World Opinion, Judge Kang A. Roo presiding. After all were seated and the gavel banging had subsided, the judge turned to the plaintiff, Robert F. Mager, and asked that the charges be summarized.

"They're all guilty, your honor," he said.

"Yes, yes, I know," replied the judge impatiently. "But I think we should at least identify the defendants and read the charges before we pass sentence. In the interests of justice, that is. Read the charges."

"Oh, all right," grumbled Mager. "But they're all guilty of tampering with the subject manuscript or its packaging in one way or another.

"The usual meliorists helped with the initial continuity check, making sure there was some sort of coherence or flow from start to finish. They insisted on wholesale changes of the first draft, leading to a lot of work. They are Dave Cram and John Warriner."

"Scoundrels," said the judge. "We'll deal with them later."

"Those who badgered me on aspects of technical consistency, leading to additional anguished effort, are Bill Deterline, Peter Pipe, Maryjane Rees, and Paul Whitmore."

"A devious sounding lot," snorted the judge.

"A whole basketful of people tested for content to make sure the desired outcome was achieved. They are Norman Carter, Ray Dargus, Margo Hicks, Jane Kilkenny, Dan McCampbell,

Tim Mossteller, Dick Niedrich, Peter Selby,
Nancy Selden, Andy Stevens, and Eileen Mager."

"Incredible," eyebrowed the judge.

"A number of souls checked to make sure
there were no unnecessary turnoffs. These
attitude checkers demanded changes to things
that slowed them down, turned them off, or
rubbed them the wrong way. They are Dale
Ball, Tom Frankum, Margo Hicks, Don DeLong,
and Pam Varga."

"You have my complete sympathy," sighed
the judge. "Is there more?"

"Yes, your honor," replied Mager. "There
are the jargon checkers who pointed to words
that were longer or more obscure than necessary, the ones who carried out my poor man's
readability test: Joanne Lackey and Katia
Prozinski."

"Such impudence will not go unpunished.
Carry on."

"There is a clump of folks who did the
title check, poking and picking at words,
inferences, and implications. They are Max
Forster, Mary Hurley, Dick Lewis, Jeanne
Mager, Laura Newmark, Charles Selden, Bill
Shanner, Jim Shearer, Charlie Spears, Hal
Chitwood, Carol Valen, Casey Williamson,
Eileen Mager, Robert Lowe, Linda Marsh, Bill
Valen, Stuart Burnett, Susan Klein, Herb
Goodyear, JoAnn Egenes, Sally Livingston,
Bruce Fredrickson, and Laurie Mandel. They
are particularly guilty."

"Oh? Why izzat?" queried the judge.

"Because they didn't like <u>MY</u> title and
made me give it up."

"Never mind. Justice will triumph."

"Finally, your honor, there are those who
hooted and hollered and stomped all over the
cover designs, trying to make sure that something agreeable to folks other than myself
would be used. They are Marshall Arky, Pete

Burt, Jim Edwards, John Feldhusen, Ollie Holt, Roger Kaufman, Kathy Keeler, Brad Mager, Randy Mager, Sue Markle, Rosalind Ruhl, Harry Shoemaker, Miriam Sierra-Franco, Bob Snyder, Wanda Sterner, Barbara Wachner, John Welser, Dee Williams, C. Glenn Valentine, and Lori Vanderschmidt. Those who tested the new cover designs were Johan Adriaanse, Gerard Conesa, Paul Guersch, David Heath, Eileen Mager, Clair Miller, Fahad Omair, Dan Piskorik, Phil Postel, Jim Reed, Ethel Robinson, Bill Valen, Carol Valen, Bob White, and Letitia Wiley. And that's the lot of them."

"Well," exclaimed the keeper of the scales. "I never! What I mean is--I never! What shall we do with them?"

"Why, we should expose them for what they are," replied Mager while fervently waggling a straightened finger. "We should place them in the pillory of public perception. We should place their names in posterity where all will be reminded of their deeds, where all will be reminded of just who was responsible for the shaping of the innards and the outards of subject manuscript. The world should know how helpful they were and that their help was appreciated."

"So ordered," gaveled the judge. "And let this be a lesson to everyone. Court's adjourned."

And it was, too.

Selected
References

Dahl, T. A. "The Measurement of Congruence between Learning Objectives and Test Items." Ph.D. dissertation, University of Michigan. University Microfilms, Ann Arbor, Michigan, 1971.

Deterline, W. A. "Testing! Testing! Testing!" *Journal of the National Society for Programmed Instruction,* Vol. X, No. 8, October 1971.

Learning Research Center. "Expecting Evaluation Excellence." *Teaching-Learning Issues,* No. 22. University of Tennessee, Knoxville, 1973.

McClelland, D. C. "Testing for Competence Rather than for 'Intelligence'." *American Psychologist,* Vol. 28, No. 1, January 1973.

*Objective/Item Checklist**

1. What performance is stated in the objective?
2. What is the performance?

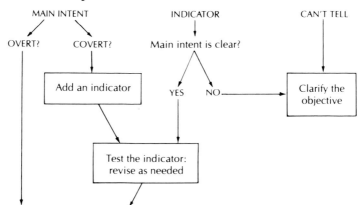

3. What overt performance is asked for by the objective?
4. What performance is asked for by the item?
5. Do the performances match?

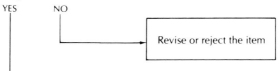

6. Do objective and item conditions match?

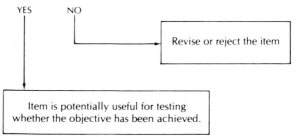

* Courtesy of Mager Associates, Inc.

Objective/Item Matching Flowchart*

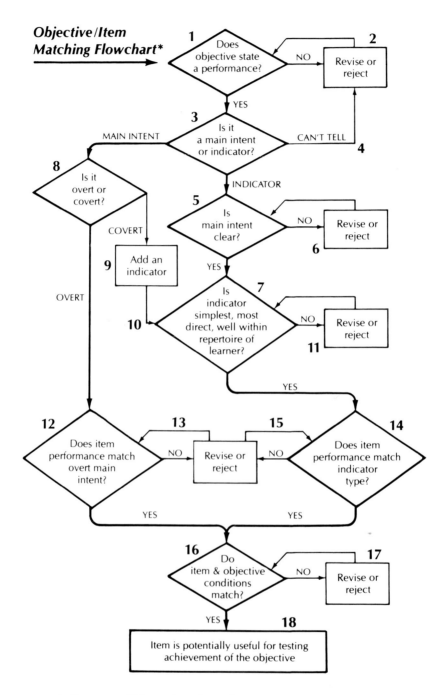

1 — Does objective state a performance? — **NO** → 2 Revise or reject

YES ↓

3 — Is it a main intent or indicator? — **CAN'T TELL** → 4

MAIN INTENT →

8 — Is it overt or covert?

INDICATOR ↓

5 — Is main intent clear? — **NO** → 6 Revise or reject

COVERT → 9 Add an indicator

YES ↓

10 — 7 Is indicator simplest, most direct, well within repertoire of learner? — **NO** → 11 Revise or reject

OVERT ↓

YES →

12 — Does item performance match overt main intent? — **NO** → 13 Revise or reject — **NO** ← 15 — 14 Does item performance match indicator type?

YES ← 13 → **YES** → 15

16 — Do item & objective conditions match? — **NO** → 17 Revise or reject

YES ↓

18 Item is potentially useful for testing achievement of the objective

* Courtesy of Mager Associates, Inc.